With Christ
The Gospel under
the Guidance of Saint Benedict

Jean-François Baudoz

LITURGICAL PRESS
Collegeville, Minnesota

www.litpress.org

From the same author:

Les miettes de la table: étude synoptique et socio-religieuse de Matthieu 15,21-28 et de Marc 7,24-30, [Crumbs from the Table: Synoptic and Socio-Religious Study of Matthew 15:21-28 and Mark 7:24-30], Paris: J. Gabalda, 1995.

Cover design by Joachim Rhoades, O.S.B. Illustration: Hans Memling (1425/40–1494), *Saint Benedict,* Uffizi, Florence, Italy. Photo credit: Scala/Art Resource, N.Y.

This book was originally published in French under the title *Avec le Christ: L'Évangile à l'école de saint Benoît* by Desclée de Brouwer in Paris, © Desclée de Brouwer 2002. All rights reserved.

1   2   3   4   5   6   7   8

Library of Congress Cataloging-in-Publication Data

Baudoz, Jean-François.
    [Avec le Christ. English]
    With Christ : the Gospel under the guidance of Saint Benedict / Jean-François Baudoz.
       p. cm.
    Includes bibliographical references.
    ISBN 13: 978-0-8146-1828-8 (pbk : alk. paper)
    ISBN 10: 0-8146-1828-6 (pbk : alk. paper)
    1. Christian life—Catholic authors. 2. Benedict, Saint, Abbot of Monte Cassino. Regula. I. Title.

BX2350.3.B3813 2005
242--dc22   2004026143

To the Monks of Tamié

Contents

Preface

The title of this work could mislead the reader into expecting to find in these pages a series of recommendations "to be with Christ." Such books, often prestigious and still fruitful, have been numerous in the past and are still numerous today. They fulfill the role they have assigned to themselves: to help women and men to become disciples of Christ. A whole life, however long, is necessary to arrive at that point, so true is it that Christian life is a journey or an apprenticeship. This is why Saint Benedict defines the monastery as a "school for the Lord's service."[1] This means that one is not born a Christian but becomes a Christian. Of course, one becomes a Christian at a precise moment in time by baptism but also by working throughout one's life on that never-ending task. Certain persons claim, not without reason, that to be a disciple belongs to the domain of art.[2] Now, it is common knowledge that two words have been used to designate those who practice art: artist and artisan. Is it not possible to compare the Christian to an artisan, conscientious like Saint Joseph? That this saint is celebrated with the title of artisan suggests that he worked at his faith in the same way he worked at his craft.

Then why this title, *With Christ*? In the first place, because of wisdom (the Latin *sapientia* is akin to the verb *sapere* which means "to taste"[3]); in the second place, because of profession (I am an exegete by trade); but above all, because I am a Christian (a term derived from the word *Christ*). As such, I assiduously

---

1. *RB 1980: The Rule of St. Benedict*, ed. Timothy Fry (Collegeville, Minn.: The Liturgical Press, 1981) Prologue, 45. All quotations from the Rule in this book are taken from this edition.

2. Père Jérôme, *L'art d'être disciple* (Paris: Le Serment/Fayard, 1989).

3. Charles Michaux, *Traces de contemplation*, Signatures (Paris: Cerf, 1998) 13.

study closely the Holy Scriptures, especially the Gospels, which I teach. Among many others, a point continues to astonish me: according to the Gospel of Mark, when Jesus "appointed twelve," it was first of all for them "to be with him" and then, only secondarily, for them "to be sent out to proclaim the message, and to have authority to cast out demons" (3:14). Because in this Gospel the distinction between the Twelve and the disciples is not clear, one can say that the primary goal for both the disciple and the apostle is *to be with* Jesus, a theme copiously exploited by the apostle Paul. "I have been crucified with Christ; and it is no longer I who live, but it is Christ who lives in me. And the life I live now in the flesh I live by faith in the Son of God, who loved me and gave himself for me" (Gal 2:19-20).

A stay of nearly one year at the Abbey of Tamié, in a community of Trappist monks, assiduous to prayer and used to hard work—(*ora et labora,* pray and work)—gave me at the same time the idea, the theme, and the form of this book. It is not a work of exegesis, but rather a series of meditations, or still more accurately, a series of thoughts fit for *lectio divina* (sacred reading). The unifying theme is Christ and more precisely this program of Christian life: *to be with Christ.* A gospel phrase, very short in most cases, orients each *lectio.* Thus my intention has been to honor a most ancient tradition in monasticism, which one of the early Cistercian fathers, William of Saint-Thierry, has, so to speak, codified in a celebrated passage: "Everyday we must also take a mouthful from the daily reading and entrust it to the stomach of memory, a passage that will be better digested and which, brought back into the mouth, will be the object of a frequent rumination."[4] For their part, the monks devote several hours of their days to *lectio.* It would be a mistake to think that these few pages are destined for the monks; even though I have on occasion given a talk to them, in fact they have been the ones who taught me.

---

4. William of Saint-Thierry, *Lettre aux frères du Mont-Dieu: lettre d'or,* Sources chrétiennes 223 (Paris: Cerf, 1975), quoted by Philippe Baud, *La ruche de Cîteaux: les plus belles pages des premiers Pères cisterciens,* Epiphanie: Tradition monastique (Paris: Cerf, 1997) 46.

Every one of the examples of *lectio divina* in this book is the fruit of personal meditations and thoughts, most often nurtured by numerous readings. One of the aims of *lectio* is to appropriate to oneself the Word of God, not to master it but to feed on it; thus, after a while one does not know exactly where the different foods come from, that is, with whom this or that comment, this or that thought originated. Which means that the pages that follow are equally the work of their author and that of other authors who strongly influenced me, even though their names are not cited in the notes. This is not because I did not want to name them but because my method, which is not academic, did not require that I mention every time from whom I borrowed such and such an idea, such and such an insight.

I said in the beginning that this book is not a manual for the disciple's use. However, may I be permitted to quote a word of advice which is not mine. Chapter 4 of the Rule of Saint Benedict, followed by Benedictines as well as Cistercians, is entitled "The Tools for Good Works." It is an enumeration of seventy-three precepts which the monks are obliged to observe. One of those precepts summarizes or concentrates them all: "The love of Christ must come before all else" (RB 4.21). Is not this the key to any Christian life, whatever form it assumes? The vocation to which we all are called is in any case *to be with Christ* for all eternity.[5]

---

5. Michel Quesnel, *L'éternité qui m'est offerte* (Paris: Desclée de Brouwer, 1998).

Chapter 1

Breaks

It is to your advantage that I go away.
John 16:7

Breaks, transitions, bereavements . . . Far from life being a long quiet river, as the title of a movie suggests, everything happens as if human life was in fact made of transitions to negotiate, thresholds to cross, bereavements to overcome; in all these our affections and attachments are pitilessly dealt with.

It is the experience of young persons, who, in order to grow, must learn to leave their families: the full realization of their lives exacts this price. It is the experience of parents, who to help their children grow (to *raise* them in the first meaning of the word), must push them out from the family circle: it is their duty and their responsibility. Everyone knows how troubling the present-day reluctance of young adults to leave the family nest is, as if social life was so hard that only the warmth of family life could temper it and make it bearable. They thus run the risk of bypassing real life, the life mentioned in the beginning of the book of Genesis, "a man leaves his father and his mother and clings to his wife, and they become one flesh" (Gen 2:24). Therefore, every affectionate relationship presupposes a distancing. Better still, in order to be fruitful every new relationship calls for a separation. Indeed, the first gesture of the Creator God was to separate the light from the darkness (Gen 1:4). Life is born from separation:

1

such is also the first event in the life of a human baby, whose coming into the world is an act of separation.

This was also the experience of Abraham, who, in order to gain the land God wanted to give him, had to leave his country, his kindred, and his father's house (Gen 12:1). It is only at this price that it was given him to become the father of believers. His fecundity was exceptional, comparable to the number of grains of sand or the number of stars in the sky, which humans have not yet succeeded in counting (Gen 15:5). It was the experience of Jesus, who, in order to go to the Father, had to be parted from his disciples. Conversely, it was the experience of the disciples, who, in order to receive the Holy Spirit (John 16:17), had to live through Jesus' death.

The occurrence of apparently unfortunate episodes, which one would be able to overcome or which one would prefer to do without, follows in fact from the necessity imposed on the human condition. What I mean here is that even though the distancing is painfully experienced, it is in truth a promise of blossoming.

It is the paradox of every human life, every Christian life, every spiritual life. This is why Jesus dares to say to his disciples, "It is to your advantage that I go away" (John 16:7). On occasion we may hear someone say, or we ourselves think, that faith in Jesus was easier for those who knew him on the roads of Galilee and saw him and heard him announce the coming of the reign of God. In fact, Jesus most often met with indifference or incomprehension and was left with only a handful of disciples, most of them unable to comprehend either his identity or his message.

Perhaps the disciples failed to understand because they lacked the end of the story, for quite often a human life needs to be completed in order to become clear and to acquire its meaning. It is probable that we already have received the painful grace of having an experience which must be spoken of with extreme reserve: it is only after loved ones have left us that we see what was best in them and understand their lives in a new way. Their absence is the source of another mode of presence because it is in the time of absence that presence becomes real and, being condensed, reaches its true reality.

★ ★ ★

On the anniversary of the death of the seven monks of Tibhirine (May 21), chance had it—or rather the established order, because in a monastery nothing is left to chance—that I was the one to proclaim the seven brothers' names at the commemoration of the dead. That was the only moment of that day when in the liturgy they were counted among the dead. Otherwise, that day was called their *dies natalis*.[1] Massacre, execution, assassination were never mentioned. The monk who was presider at the Eucharist, a friend of Brother Christopher,[2] soberly compared their death to Christ's: the historical circumstances of Jesus' crucifixion do not explain the mystery of Redemption; in the same way, the circumstances of the death of the brothers of Tibhirine do not explain the mystery of their life or of their death. I remember the exceptional impact of that Eucharist; it was not due only to emotion. Beyond their death and because of it, the brothers' presence was beyond the boundaries of what can be expressed, a presence at the very core of this absence. I believe that this is what we call the communion of saints.

John's Gospel precisely helps us to understand that it was necessary that Jesus should die, that his life derived its meaning only through its completion, and that his absence was the cause of another type of presence generating even greater riches.

What are those riches? According to John 14:23-26, where no limit is assigned to their number, they are the words of Jesus and of the Holy Spirit. And one must immediately add that we do not have here two realities foreign to one another, for one of the functions of the Holy Spirit is precisely to make us remember

1. According to a most ancient Christian tradition, the day of death is called *dies natalis* (birthday).

2. Christophe, moine de Tibhirine, *Le souffle du don: Journal de frère Christophe, moine de Tibhirine, 8 août 1993–19 mars 1996* (Paris: Bayard/Centurion, 1999) 2.

Jesus' word: "Those who love me will keep my word. . . . The Advocate, the Holy Spirit, whom the Father will send in my name, will teach you everything, and remind you of all that I have said to you."

A document from the Congregation for the Doctrine of the Faith rightly reminded us that "the full and complete revelation of the mystery . . . of God is realized in Jesus Christ (*Dominus Jesus,* par. 6). However, Jesus did not say everything: his words do not exhaust his word, that is to say, the contents of his message. This is precisely the reason he asks his disciples—he asks us—to remain faithful to his word, since he himself is the Word: "In the beginning was the Word, and the Word was with God, and the Word was God" (John 1:1). To be faithful to Jesus' word is to live by his Spirit, the gift he gave us.

It is with good reasons that the Church both venerates and ponders the words of Holy Scripture. But it is in order to cause the Spirit to arise so that this word, now Scripture, may become light for those who listen to it and practice it. The only way to keep the word of Christ is to live by it. If we do not live by it, it is a dead letter; it is good only to gather dust on the shelves of some library. Sometimes it is said that the Christian religion is among the religions of the Book. Nothing more erroneous! The Christian religion does not venerate a book. It acclaims and proclaims a Word, Christ, who is living today and who today speaks in his Church.

Contrary to those who followed Jesus on the roads of Palestine, we have seen or heard nothing. But we do have a great advantage over the disciples before Easter: we know the final word, we know that the mystery of the death and resurrection of Jesus opens for us the way to eternity. And when waiting for the coming of this eternal reign, it is granted us to taste the real presence of Jesus in the Eucharist: "Blessed are those who are invited to the marriage supper of the Lamb" (Rev 19:9).

Chapter 2

Temptations

If you are the Son of God.
Luke 4:3

We were crossing the desert of Sinai. Even though it is possible in our day to go through it much more quickly than the people of Israel, traveling on foot only, weariness soon takes hold of you due to the lack of comfort and to the heat. Rudimentary conditions of life, added to the feeling of strangeness, heavily tax your physical and psychological resistance. Had the person in charge miscalculated what would be needed on this particular day? In any case, we were submitted to a severe rationing of food, each person being allotted only one or two pieces of bread. Things became even worse when we were told not to waste water because the reserve was extremely low. We knew of course that water is precious in the desert: it is used to quench one's thirst and not to wash oneself. Already tired, might we have misunderstood? or taken literally what was only a warning? In any case, discontent insidiously set in among us. I still can see us, a few friends and I sitting in the shade of one of the four-wheel drives; it was not an open rebellion but a latent dissatisfaction, which is worse. We murmured against the person in charge, against the situation, against everything. We murmured because we were tempted by the desire for abundant food, cool water springing forth from the rock, and untroubled rest. The environment and the circumstances were too much like the episode of the mumbling of the people during the Exodus (Exod 15:22-25; 16:1-3) for the similarity not to become evident to us. Which immediately relaxed the tension. I regard this experience, obviously caricatural but true, as the illustration of every temptation, at the root of which there is always dissatisfaction to a lesser or greater degree. Without a doubt, this is the reason St. Benedict warns monastics against murmuring: "First and foremost, there must be no word or sign of the evil of grumbling, no manifestation of it for any reason at all" (RB 34.6).

★ ★ ★

The desert is the place of trial where self-defense does not function any longer, where, unprotected, we find ourselves facing ourselves, facing God. This is why it is also the privileged place of the encounter with God: "Therefore, I will now allure her, / and bring her into the wilderness, / and speak tenderly to her" (Hos 2:14). We do not escape the experience of the desert any more than the people of Israel did: desert of solitude or anguish, desert of our cities or relationships, desert of our trials, our doubts, and our disappointments.

But if we read the account of Jesus' temptations (Matt 4:1-11; Mark 1:12-13; Luke 4:1-13), we see ourselves invited to go to the desert of our own accord, led by the Holy Spirit. We are invited to live the trial of trust and faithfulness. But if we are pushed into the desert, we are not going there alone because we are the disciples of the one who has gone before us and waits for us there: Christ. Let us make no mistake; the Gospel makes us contemplate Jesus challenged by the mystery of temptation and evil—for it is necessary to contemplate it first—so that we may find the courage to face, in our turn, the struggle of the desert, that is, the struggle of life against death, of truth against lie, of reality against illusion.

★ ★ ★

Let us contemplate Christ in his struggle.

"If you are the Son of God. . . ." It is in his deepest and truest identity that Jesus is tempted. And the devil challenges Jesus. "*If* you are the Son of God. . . ." In this *if* it is faith which is at stake . . . and first that of Jesus. Because, in his case, to change stones into bread and jump down from the pinnacle of the temple were only the expression of the real temptation which he often had to fight: that of taking advantage of the title of Son of God in order to work miracles that would clearly manifest who he was. To manifest through miracles that he was the Son of God would amount to Jesus' succumbing to the fundamental temptation, the one Adam and Eve did not resist: to become "like God" (Gen 3:5), that is, to decide everything with sovereign power, declare where good is and where evil is, deny one's own humanity in order to raise oneself by one's own strength to the point of becoming like God.

For Jesus, as for us, the only true temptation consists in placing ourselves as rivals of God instead of recognizing that we are sons and daughters of God. To claim complete independence from God, to want to master life and death—as if life was not first of all a gift, this is the permanent temptation. This is the Promethean dream of humankind, however impossible it is to realize it to the end even though science and technology make new progress everyday.

Perhaps we are thinking that at our personal level the problem does not present itself in terms as categorical and that rare are the times when we have the opportunity, that is, the temptation, to choose for or against God. This is true; however, we all know that Christian life is not lived apart from ordinary life and that it functions in the banality of daily existence. To want at any cost to impose one's own will, to selfishly choose oneself, these are the temptations which we must face everyday. Choosing oneself is tantamount to preferring one's own will to God's.

In Saint Benedict's eyes, nothing is worse than self-will. On several occasions, he insists on that point in his Rule. Experienced in both humanity and spirituality, the lawgiver of monastics knows well that self-will is the main obstacle standing in their way. Thus, in chapter 7 of the Rule, which deals with humility, he writes: "The second step of humility is that a man loves not his own will, nor takes pleasure in the satisfaction of his own desires; rather he shall imitate by his actions that saying of the Lord: *I came not to do my own will, but the will of him who sent me*" (*RB* 7.31-32). Now this quote from John 6:38 was already used in chapter 5, which deals with obedience. This insistence calls for our asking the question: Does the renunciation of one's own will concern only monastics? Of course not. First of all it concerns all Christians since all disciples without exception must imitate their Master. Not without reason is the doing of God's will one of the Beatitudes in Luke's Gospel: "Blessed rather are those who hear the word of God and obey it" (Luke 11:28).

★ ★ ★

Let us continue to contemplate Christ. Christ, the Son of God from all eternity, responds to the devil's suggestion not by appealing to his divinity. Rather, he draws his answer from his humanity, which at its deepest and truest level has an absolute need of bread to live, precisely in order to recognize that bread is not sufficient. Human beings live on bread but do "not live by bread alone." Fully human, the Son of God proclaims that humanity by itself is not the totality of human beings.

And this concerns us to the highest degree. For Christ, as for us, there is no possible answer to temptation, whatever it may be, without our most earthly humanity, that is, without our heart and body. Any other response, for example that coming from the imagination, is illusory.

In this desert, which we are always called to cross, in one way or another, it is true that allowing ourselves to be mastered by a banal temptation is not by itself posing ourselves as rivals of God. This being said, resisting an apparently insignificant temptation can be the sign and maybe the whole reason for the war I wage against myself and my selfishness, that is, the war I wage for God. In fact, the heart of the matter is not to practice asceticism for itself but to make of it the sign of the place we accord to God in our lives. For example, resisting the temptation of food can be the sign that I am not dominated by what I nonetheless need in order to live.

★ ★ ★

It may be that we dream of escaping temptation. But precisely, this is only a dream. Even Jesus had to confront hunger, pride, the desire for power and immediate satisfaction. It is precisely because he has assumed the trial of temptation that he teaches his disciples to say, "Lead us not into temptation." By this plea we do not ask God to be spared every form of temptation. We ask God to help us not to be dominated by it. In any case, saying to God, "Lead us not into temptation" (Matt 6:13; Luke 11:4), is to recognize that we are his children since this request follows the invocation "Our Father who art in heaven."

The whole undertaking is not without consequence because if we recognize that we are children of God, we accept the risk of hearing these words addressed to us, "If you are the child of God. . . ." And it is precisely there that our struggle takes place because it is there that, like Christ quoting Scripture, we testify to the fact that human beings do not live by bread alone but also by the bread of his word and of his body.

"Father, do not bring us to the time of trial!" (see Luke 11:4).

Chapter 3

Martyrs

He loved them to the end.
John 13:1

"I give you a new commandment, that you love one another. Just as I have loved you, you also should love one another" (John 13:34).

In the Fourth Gospel these are the opening words of Jesus' farewell discourse. It follows the washing of the feet (13:1–20), defined as an "example" to be followed (13:15), and the betrayal (13:21–30) by Judas who was not permitted to hear the new commandment: even though he took part in the washing of the feet, he did not let his heart be purified by the Lord and Master, who declared, "You are clean though not all of you" (13:10). If indeed "it was night" (13:30), that night was first in Judas' heart.

★ ★ ★

Thus, the distinctive sign of Christians is not external, because love comes from the heart. According to the Fourth Gospel, to love is even the only necessary condition to be truly a disciple of Jesus: "By this everyone will know that you are my disciples, if you have love for one another" (John 13:35). Is not this word at once marvelous and fearsome?

Marvelous, because, immediately following the new commandment, it obliges us to go to the very roots of faith, that is, to keep the memorial of the One who died because of love: "Having loved his own who were in the world, he loved them to the end" (John 13:1). And we know that memorial is more than mere remembrance. It is an actualization of the death and resurrection of the Lord, including the washing of the feet.

Fearsome, because those who see how we live should discover we are Christians thanks to the love we manifest and which is the very love of Christ who loved us to the extreme. Of course, I know that love is not the monopoly of Christians. Fortunately, it is possible to love others without being Jesus' disciple. From that point of view, the Christians' only privilege is the possibility of recognizing the source of love and naming it. Love (1 John 4:8), Spirit (John 4:24), and Light (1 John 1:5) are the three names given to God in the Johannine corpus.

"Love one another as I have loved you" (John 15:12). This command is called "new" in the Fourth Gospel; what is the nature of this newness?

For Jesus, love is no longer an option, but becomes a command. It is the law that rules the life of those who claim to be Jesus' disciples. It would be an error to classify this law among other laws; it contains all the particular precepts which the Fourth Gospel, in contradistinction to the Synoptics, avoids specifying. The locution "new commandment" must be understood both as an ethical imperative and as the *mandate* of the Father which Jesus transmits to us: "The Father who sent me has himself given me a commandment about what to say and what to speak. And I know that his commandment is eternal life. What I speak, therefore, I speak just as the Father has told me" (John 12:49-50).

There is another newness which concerns the way of loving. The commandment is not restricted to a demand of love; it also defines its modality. We must love *like* Christ. This means we must love *as much as* I have loved you, *in the measure* I have loved you, and *because* I have loved you. However, the demand is not arbitrary: if the disciples' love is founded on the love of Christ for them, it is the love of the Father for the Son which is the original source: "As the Father has loved me, so I have loved you; abide in my love" (John 15:9). Fraternal love is thus image and likeness of the Father's love for the Son. It is our duty not to distort either, but at the same time, we must remember that since fraternal love has its origin in God, it is a grace as much as an imperative.

★ ★ ★

How shall we live this grace? More precisely *How far to follow?*—according to the title of the book written by Dom Bernardo Olivera after the death of the seven monks of Tibhirine.[1] By choosing this title, the abbot general of the Cistercians–Trappists was alluding, I think, to a question put by Brother Paul a little over one year before the abduction: "How far can you go to save yourself without running the risk of losing true life: only one Person knows the day and the hour of our liberation in him. . . . We should be open to his action in our lives by prayer and loving presence to all our brothers."[2]

Must we underscore why this declaration is remarkable? As soon as the question is posed, the answer is given: nothing is worth anything except the love of God, which is expressed in prayer, and except the love of the brothers and sisters, which is expressed by a loving presence. Together with the other six monks, Brother Paul has sealed this conviction with his blood.

I did not know personally any of the seven brothers of the Atlas. But the abbey which welcomed me for a few months is the one where two among them, Brother Christopher and Brother Paul, made their monastic profession and lived several years before leaving for Algeria. I feel a certain connection with them because I heard a lot about them and because their brothers have become mine.

---

1. Bernardo Olivera, *How Far to Follow?: The Martyrs of Atlas* (Kalamazoo, Mich.: Cistercian Publications, 1997).
2. Quoted by Olivera, ibid., 9.

They have made me realize the proximity of martyrdom. Since it was given me to live everyday and in the same place the life that a few years earlier they had lived in silence and humility (office, prayer, *lectio*, work), I often thought that nothing had predisposed them to the day and the hour of their passage into Life. Thanks to them, I have understood that even though martyrdom remains exceptional, it is, however, part and parcel of the Christian vocation. Up to the moment of the supreme trial, those who will become martyrs are ordinary Christians, as Bernardo Olivera writes in his presentation of the seven brothers: "A group like so many others we can meet in our monasteries or parishes or on the streets of our cities Some were withdrawn, others communicative. Some were placid, others highly emotional. Some were more inclined to intellectual work, others to manual work. What united them was their search for God in community, their love for the Algerian people, and a bond of unbreakable fidelity with the pilgrim church in Algeria."[3]

I can no longer pray Psalm 101 without recalling the last words of Brother Christopher's Journal before the abduction on March 19, the feast of Saint Joseph: "I have, as it were, heard Joseph's voice inviting me to sing Psalm 101 with him and the child: 'I will sing of loyalty and of justice. . . . I will study the way that is blameless. / When shall I attain it? / I will walk with integrity of heart' (vv. 1-2)."[4]

He has walked with integrity of heart with those of his house; that is to say, he has loved to the end (John 13:1).

If I speak of martyrdom—in Greek this means testimony—in connection with the brothers of Tibhirine, it is not just because I admire them. It is also to contemplate the serene power of the love "to the end." There was neither fanaticism nor ostentation among those brothers. Without a doubt, they foresaw where their unanimous decision to remain in Tibhirine would lead them. They took the risk of having inscribed in their flesh

---

3. Ibid.

4. Christophe, moine de Tibhirine, *Le souffle du don: Journal de frère Christophe, moine de Tibhirine, 8 août 1993–19 mars 1996* (Paris: Bayard/Centurion, 1999) 204.

the word, "We know love by this that he laid down his life for us—and we ought to lay down our lives for one another" (1 John 3:16). *How far to go?* is the question every disciple of Christ is justified in asking. *To the end* is the answer given by the Gospel. Our brothers of the Atlas have given this answer in its pure radicalness; the same answer is demanded of us. *Like* Jesus, they have shown us the way.

Chapter 4

Identity and Otherness

Is not this Joseph's son?
Luke 4:22

For several years a book periodically comes back on the market; its title varies but little, "For you, who is Jesus Christ?" Must we see in this a sign of the interest shown, if not for Jesus as "Jesus Christ, the Son of God" (Mark 1:1), at least for his message? In our day, most people have a certain sympathy for a person who, provided one has heard of him (see Mark 7:25), can appear fascinating because of his actions and even more because of his words.

Although I don't know with any certainty why these books are so successful, I see clearly that the answers show little variation from one decade to the next, whether they come from known personalities, politicians, writers, artists, bishops . . . or from anonymous responders, Christians or non-Christians. Either Jesus is defined in the terms of the Creed or he is seen as a man who left a message of universal fraternity. I think that we should be surprised neither by the sameness of the answers nor by their extreme diversity. Jesus' figure is eminently malleable and it is very easy to subject it to a variety of projections, from the most sophisticated to the less complex, from those akin to confessions of faith to those much less dogmatic in content.

The most intriguing point in all this is that the Gospels are not much help in resolving these contradictions. One realizes that in all these answers, the readers find the Jesus they seek: the implacable judge (Matt 25:12) or the merciful one (Matt 5:5), the one who knows everything (John 5:21) or the one who does not know the hour of the end of time (Mark 13:32), the one who is powerful in words and acts (Acts 10:38) or the one whose weakness leads him to the cross (Phil 2:6).

★ ★ ★

In the scene where Luke describes Jesus in the synagogue of Nazareth, we see his neighbors wondering, "Is not this Joseph's son?" They have an idea of Jesus which is certainly not accurate. But let us beware of blaming them for this: many other persons in the Gospel, including some important ones, have groped before grasping Jesus' true identity. Before being named "the Messiah of God" by Peter in the same Gospel (Luke 9:20), Jesus had been believed to be John the Baptist, Elijah, one of the ancient prophets (9:19). The fault of the people of Nazareth was not so much to make an error concerning Jesus' identity than to lock him up in the categories they knew. They thus imprisoned him in a person that he was not. Of course, it could be pointed out that we have here not a statement but a question, "Is not this Joseph's son?" But the interrogative form is used only to underscore the Nazarenes' astonishment; it does not question their conviction.

One can see the risk here: a messiah being Joseph's son would be only the messiah of Nazareth, a local prophet. But Jesus is "the Messiah, the Lord," according to the message delivered by the angels at Bethlehem (Luke 2:11; see Acts 2:36), that is the Other, the one who, although a human, also has his origin in God.

It is probably because their remark shows them prisoners of their limited human views that Jesus retorts, "Doubtless you will quote to me this proverb, 'Doctor, cure yourself'" (Luke 4:23). Jesus breaks down their boundaries so as to open new horizons, those of Sidon and Syria, that is to say, the horizons, both surprising and unexpected, of the pagan nations: "There were many widows in Israel in the time of Elijah, when the heaven was shut up three years and six months, and there was a severe famine over all the land; yet Elijah was sent to none of them except to a widow at Zarephath in Sidon. There were also many lepers in Israel in the time of the prophet Elisha, and none of them was cleansed except Naaman the Syrian" (Luke 4:25-27).

In any case, this gospel page shows how difficult it is to recognize the other in his or her true identity; spontaneously we assimilate others to the images we have of them.

★ ★ ★

In order to start my car, stopped in front of an abbey, I was forced to appeal to the brother in charge of the door, who in turn went for a monk expert in mechanics. The clock on the church steeple marked 12:30 PM, and for a monk, as for the majority of people, it is lunchtime. To bring another vehicle, to recharge the battery, this is the classic but time-consuming scenario. Up to now, there was in all this nothing extraordinary; it was a scene of daily life.

With sincere politeness, I was expressing to this monk—whom I did not know and who did not know me—my embarrassment at imposing on him, especially at the time of the community meal. Perhaps because my excuses annoyed him, but with a frankness at least equal to mine, he retorted without preamble, "For me, at this time you are Christ."

I knew well that by saying this, the brother was only quoting a passage from the Rule of Benedict: *All guests who present themselves are to be welcomed as Christ* (53.1). Just the same, it was the first time that I was told by someone that in his eyes I represented Christ. This sort of thing takes your breath away; such a response obviously silences all your flat excuses.

When two or three years later I entered the community as a retreatant, I had the opportunity to know this monk better. Apparently and probably in reality, this monk was neither holier nor less holy than any other. Simply on that day, in that precise set of circumstances, he behaved like a genuine disciple of

Benedict and, by the same token, as a genuine disciple of Christ: "Just as you did to one of the least of these who are members of my family, you did it to me" (Matt 25:40).

I remember that in the beginnings of my stay at the monastery, I felt first charmed—novelty is always charming—and rather quickly annoyed by the thoughtful way the brothers acted toward me. I told myself that in this beginning period, they wanted to facilitate my integration into the community and that by the well-known process of weariness, their attentiveness would fade away sooner or later. But it showed no sign of lessening and it began to mightily exercise me: it was impossible to hold a sheet of paper without someone immediately taking it from you; impossible to go and wash your own eating implements without someone instantly doing it for you; impossible to turn the pages of your psalter without your neighbor in choir[1] hurrying to show you the right page. People being charitable toward me I could accept, but people meddling with my own business was insufferable. The day I opened my eyes and looked not just at myself but at other people helped me to take one important step: I noted that the brothers were not preoccupied with my person, but that they were extremely thoughtful toward everyone. So at times I was enchanted—*How very good and pleasant it is when kindred live together in unity* (Ps 133:1)— at other times irritated beyond words—common life is a peck of troubles. When finally and suddenly Benedict's phrase *to receive the other as Christ* made sense to me, everything became clear. Of course, annoyances both petty and secret did not disappear, but I was now able to relativize them.

To do something in the place of another, something the other could do without problem is no favor to that person, if one judges by the standards of useful and useless. In reality such an act is purely gratuitous; it shows to other persons that I do not ignore them, that they exist for me, that they are those

---

1. In the church of an a monastery, the choir designates the place which the monastics occupy (most often in stalls).

without whom I could not live and who cannot live without me. To use Christian terms, others have for me the face of Christ; I cannot pass them by without seeing them and without manifesting to them that I recognize them as brothers and sisters in Christ.

★ ★ ★

What has all this to do with the scene in the synagogue of Nazareth?

I can take the other for *Joseph's son*, that is, make a mistake as to the other's deep identity; I can see in others only what they allow to be seen and what very often offends and displeases me. To classify others in a known category is then a way of reassuring myself because I am so afraid of others. In effect, they oblige me to look at myself through them: this is the reason why I feel inclined to project on them the dark zones which I do not want to see in myself. Hence the irritations and aggravations.

There is another way of looking at others, a way that places me in the presence of the Other, that is, the mystery of God who took for us a human face in the features of Jesus of Nazareth.

It is true that the problems and difficulties arising in relationships are not thereby resolved as if by magic: we remain, thanks be to God, human through and through. But to welcome the other as Christ completely upsets our usual way of seeing, by opening unsuspected horizons, those of Syria and the land of Sidon (see Luke 4:25-27).

Chapter 5

Identity and Recognition

Do you love me?
John 21:15

Chapter 21 of John's Gospel appears to have no connection whatsoever with the account of the paschal appearances of Christ in chapter 20. And this is not for literary reasons only.[1] Ordinariness has reclaimed its rights: the horizon of Galilee has closed back in upon itself; the lake is henceforth just a place to fish, and Peter, the fisherman, feels the desire to return to his trade. The others follow him and repeat the ritual gestures with the boat and net only to end up in failure: "That night they caught nothing." Human hope, human disappointment. Nothing unusual here: it is a symbolic representation of the human condition.

★ ★ ★

However Jesus was there, but they did not know it. He stood on the beach (John 21:4) and without setting foot in the water,

---

1. For literary and theological reasons, scripture scholars agree that chapter 21 is a later addition to John's Gospel.

he asked them whether they had anything to eat, "Children, you have no fish, have you?" (21:5). He the Crucified and Risen One, whose hour of the Cross was the hour of glorification (John 7:39), here he was on the shore of eternity preparing ordinary human food. The Risen One would like to make his daily bread out of the ordinariness of our lives because, from the depth and the nearness of his eternity, he desires nothing else but us. In his commentary on the phrase from the Canticle, "I sought him whom my soul loves" (Cant 3:1), Saint Bernard writes, "The soul seeks the Word but it is the Word that sought it first."[2] The human quest is always preceded by the Word's quest for human beings. Bernard even sees there one of the main reasons for the Incarnation. God became human in order to offer humans a humanity to love since they had become insensitive to spiritual realities because of sin (Song of Songs, Sermon 20.6). How could the Risen One not bring to its completion this search for humanity which God undertook from the time of creation?

Jesus begs his bread, but the disciples hear only an unfamiliar voice which does not evoke any recognition. He even tells them to throw the net on the right side of the boat, advice they follow, but without understanding.

This lack of recognition lasts until the net suddenly sinks under the weight of the fish and until one single person, the one Jesus loved, perceives the identity of the stranger, "It is the Lord!" (21:7). The one who is loved is the one who recognizes him. Recognition and thankfulness come from love, and only love can remove the veil of daily ordinariness and sense and divine Jesus' presence.

In any event, it is the Beloved Disciple's voice which first causes Peter then all the others to recognize the Lord: "Now none of the disciples dared to ask him, 'Who are you?' because they knew it was the Lord" (21:12). The reason the disciples do

2. Bernard of Clairvaux, *Song of Songs*, 4 vols., trans. Kilian Walsh and Irene Edmonds, Cistercian Fathers nos. 4, 7, 31, 40 (Kalamazoo, Mich.: Cistercian Publications, 1979–1983).

not ask Jesus, is that faith does not happen in answer to questions, as if it were their culmination or their crowning. The contrary is true: it is because faith starts with recognition that it seeks to understand (*fides quaerens intellectum*, faith seeking understanding), according to Saint Anselm's fine expression.

★ ★ ★

Let us go back to the person of Peter. "It is the Lord" (21:7). The first one to follow the Beloved Disciple without the least hesitation is Peter. He trusts the one who is loved.

In other terms, it is thanks to the eyes, heart, and faith of John, the beloved disciple,[3] that the whole Church, through Peter's diving into the water, confesses that Jesus is the Lord. Because the disciple par excellence led him to discover Jesus' identity, Peter, that is, the Church, testifies that he is risen: this is his role and function.

As a consequence, there is no church without disciples contemplating Christ. Conversely, there are no genuine disciples without a church within which to contemplate the Lord.

For if it is from John that Peter learns that it is Jesus, it is precisely because John chose Peter to share his discovery. This means that John pronounces his profession of faith within the Church, represented by Peter. Bringing the net, that is, the Church, ashore without tearing it is the duty that devolves on Peter: "Peter went aboard and hauled the net ashore full of large fish, a hundred fifty-three of them; and though there were so many, the net was not torn" (21:11).

To each one his or her function.

Nevertheless, we must beware of facile classifications, for instance, associating John uniquely with love and contemplation and Peter uniquely with government and proper functioning of the institution. Because from now on only love matters. There will be no other power than that of love.

3. Tradition identifies the Beloved Disciple with John, the son of Zebedee, to whom the writing of the Gospel of John is attributed.

In the second part of John 21, Jesus does not ask Peter what his pastoral projects are. Not that these are unnecessary. But Jesus' question is first of all a request for love: "Simon, son of John, do you love me more than these?" (21:15). Three times the question is asked, echoing the threefold denial (John 18:17, 25, 27). Peter answers twice "Yes, Lord, you know that I love you" (21:15 and 16). The third time he says, "Lord, you know everything; you know that I love you" (21:17). Nothing is ever desperate, but nothing is ever ignored either. Rather than remaining silent about his disciple's denial, Jesus uses it as a device allowing Peter to better draw his strength from his Lord. Jesus uses it as a way of letting Peter draw his strength more completely from his Lord.

Humility and contrition characterize Peter's response. He confesses his weakness because he knows Jesus' immeasurable forgiveness. There is no other power than forgiven love, a love that itself will generate forgiveness. Love is true love only after having been purified by overcoming the trial.

★ ★ ★

In some monasteries it is the superior's task to give a commentary everyday on a chapter of the Rule according to a well-established calendar. No doubt this would soon grow tiring for the communities and repetitious for the superiors if they limited themselves to giving a timeless teaching. The goal of the "Chapter" is precisely to give the superiors the opportunity to interpret the Rule in a timely way in relation to their communities, their present state of mind, and their concerns, but also in relation to the events occurring in the world and the Church. It is a pastoral task in which the superiors imitate the merciful example of the Good Shepherd (see RB 27.8) by exhortation, reprimand, and encouragement. In the discharge of this exercise, there is a peculiarly difficult moment for them: they must also comment on the chapters of the Rule which deal with themselves. And, in fact, the obligation is quasi-permanent. Saint Benedict defines the superior's function in chapter 2 but comes back to the subject several times (chs. 27, 64) and in many cases trusts the superior's discernment: since the Rule cannot codify everything, when a problem needs a solution, it is for the abbot "to decide" or "to choose." One must recognize that Saint Benedict gives the abbot a considerable role, to the point that he defines monastic life as a service "under a rule and an abbot" (RB 1.2), the latter being equal to the former.

In RB 2.1-3 we read these words: "To be worthy of the task of governing a monastery, the abbot must always remember what his title signifies and act as a superior should. He is believed to hold the place of Christ in the monastery, since he is addressed by a title of Christ, as the Apostle indicates: *You have received the spirit of adoption of sons by which we exclaim, abba, father*" (see Rom 8:15). Therefore the abbot is from the beginning defined as a father, but—and this is a remarkable point—the Rule immediately adds that he must constantly remember this. And a little further on in the same chapter Benedict repeats the same expression, "The abbot must always remember what he is and remember what he is called, aware that more will be expected of a man to whom more has been entrusted" (RB 2.30).

There is no doubt that the demands of the Rule concerning the superior can frighten some people. However, it seems to me that these demands do not give a complete description of the superior's function. I myself have been by turns the witness and the beneficiary of this function, and I believe that the essential point of the Rule regarding superiors is suggested by this advice, "Let him strive to be loved rather than feared" (RB 64.15). Not by demagogy of course—Saint Benedict knows neither the word nor the practice—but by a sort of theological necessity, because *only love is worthy of being trusted*. To say it another way, to the one to whom he grants all powers, Benedict signifies that all these will be of no avail if superiors themselves do not begin by loving and accepting to be loved. Conversely, in the next to last chapter of the Rule he imposes on the monastics the duty of loving their superior "with unfeigned and humble love" (RB 72.10).

It is well known that every authority in the Church must be regarded as a service. Without, of course, excluding this aspect, chapter 21 of John's Gospel shows that any exercise of an ecclesial function is sterile unless it has love for its foundation. Benedict makes no mistake: the one given full authority over the whole monastery must behave like the Good Shepherd, full of tenderness, who loves his sheep and brings them back to the fold (RB 27.8-9). In other words, the measure in which superiors love those entrusted to their care will be the measure in which they will acknowledge them as mother or father. This will not prevent the superiors from exercising with discernment the constraints their charge entails. We understand even better why Benedict demands that superiors remember the name they are called by: their name of mother or father exacts of them both a state of mind and appropriate actions.

So when monastics listen to their superiors commenting on the chapters of the Rule, including those which concern their office, the superiors can speak to them freely, if not without fear.[4] By the fact that they listen, the monastics attest that they recognize the superiors as the mother and father of the community, and by their words, the superiors exercise a charge which they receive constantly from their hearers. It is then that they remember the name they bear.

★ ★ ★

Peter, John, the other disciples are many various and complementary figures in the Church. They have in common a recognition of the identity of the Lord, caused by love and attested in the assembly.

"They knew it was the Lord" (John 21:12). We too know that he is the Lord, even though we sometimes have a hard time recognizing him when he calls to us from the shore, especially when we have spent the whole night without catching anything.

---

4. In the Rule of Saint Benedict, as well as in the Bible, fear implies respect and love. It is not synonymous with dread or fright.

Chapter 6

End Times, Incarnation, and Present Time

When the Son of Man comes, will he find faith on earth?

Luke 18:8

Dare I say it? There are some passages of the Gospels that frighten me. Thus this word of Jesus in John's Gospel, "You search the scriptures. . . . But I know that you do not have the love of God in you" (John 5:39, 42). Personally, this reproach, which Jesus addresses to the Jews, touches me deeply. Because I am an exegete by profession, I always fear to be a good technician of the Word of God while not having the love of God in my heart.

And then there is this question put by Jesus in Luke's Gospel, "When the Son of Man comes, will he find faith on the earth?" (Luke 18:8). I do know that Jesus' question is a rather classic one in apocalyptic literature. Nonetheless I regard it as dreadful inasmuch as it suggests that there is no guarantee as to the future of the Christian faith.

26

★ ★ ★

Jesus' question concerning the state of humanity when the Son of Man returns resonates with the uncertainty of many of our contemporaries: "What will tomorrow be like?" This is the haunting question all generations have asked, but it is asked in a more urgent way in our time when our humanity seems to wander wherever the winds blow. Where indeed does our humanity go, threatened as it is by the consequences of its own discoveries? Whether we speak of pollution, of genetic manipulation, of cloning, the anguish is the greater because of all the possibilities made available by science and technology. And it is most tempting for human beings to play the sorcerer's apprentices, to pretend to replace the creator and master of life. We do not even speak of the violence rife everywhere, for example, the violence of young people who are unable to rein in their aggression because they were not taught how to exercise their freedom and responsibility. And we do not even speak of the terrorist acts which exceed what could be imagined.

In this context, some people want to see through the uncertainties of the future and assuage their anguish by consulting horoscopes and by placing a trust as unshakable as it is undeserved in astrologers of all stripes, who use and abuse the credulity of their customers. Simply, they forget that the future is not to be read but constructed, that every trail is not blazed in advance, and that human freedom plays an important role in what tomorrow will be like.

Someone else seems to have been in a similar frame of mind, the one who had asked Jesus on his way to Jerusalem, "Lord, will only a few be saved?" (Luke 13:23). As if the number of the saved was determined in advance! The question reveals someone who wants to know so as to be able to quantify and measure. That person forgets that our salvation is neither determined from always nor decided tomorrow. What must be lived is the today of God. The question is not to know whether there will be many saved tomorrow. Rather, what is important is for us to ask ourselves whether our behavior of today is consonant with the way of salvation. This is why Jesus does not answer the questioner directly; instead, he exhorts him to attend to the present: "Strive to enter through the narrow door; for many, I tell you, will try to enter and will not be able" (Luke 13:23-24).

★ ★ ★

Why enter through the narrow door? In the Sermon on the Mount (Matthew 5–7), Matthew, following his own viewpoint, is more explicit: "Enter through the narrow gate; for the gate is wide and the road is easy that leads to destruction, and there are many who take it. For the gate is narrow and the road is hard that leads to life, and there are few who find it" (Matt 7:13-14). Is not Jesus himself the door of the kingdom? If it is narrow it is not because its dimensions do not allow many to go through it. "The door is narrow" means that to enter through it entails some demands. We can illustrate this saying by two parables taken from Matthew's Gospel.

The first one is that of the wedding banquet (Matt 22:1-14). God sends the Son to conclude an alliance with humanity and those invited are many. Probably these represent the heirs by birthright, that is, the people of the first covenant. But these people excuse themselves; they have better things to do. One goes "to his farm, another to his business. . . ." (Matt 22:5). Is not this attitude that of many of our contemporaries? God liberally invites humans to enter the kingdom but humans are often deaf or else refuse to hear. Life is so encumbered that there is no place left for God.

But is not this story of the guests who decline the invitation the story of each and every one of us? In other words, when we were on the main streets and in the back alleys, we were invited to the banquet hall (22:9) without any merit on our part. But did we take care to put on the wedding garment (22:11-12)? Here Matthew speaks categorically: to be admitted to the wedding banquet, it is not enough to rely on having one's name on the guest list. Besides, one must put on the wedding robe, that is, accomplish the good works of whose importance Matthew loves to remind us (5:16-20; 7:21-22).

This lesson of the parable does not aim at making us fearful. Overall and in particular in each of its passages, the Gospel is to be received as the Good News it is. So what is the point of the parable of the wedding banquet? God calls all humans to salvation, the bad and the good (Matt 22:10). And for entering the wedding hall, being good is no more qualification than being bad is disqualification. Now this is apt to turn on their head our categories and ways of thinking. But God's logic is not our logic. May we Christians beware of regarding as a right the gift we have received. We know that we are called through God's generosity. But "Christian" is not necessarily a synonym of "elect," because only God is the judge of the conversion we have undertaken. "For many are called, but few are chosen" (Matt 22:14). This saying is not meant to establish a fatalistic predestination; it only aims at making us squarely face our responsibilities. We are saved by grace, yes, but we are not saved without ourselves.

The second parable is that of the Last Judgment (Matt 25:31-46). Here we are on the last day and the setting is as formal as it is impressive. All the nations are assembled, which means that not only Christians but all humans, whatever their belief or nonbelief. What is going to be on the agenda that day? Not the so-called important events in our lives, those which brought us honors or thanks, but unnoticed episodes, humble and fleeting moments we hardly even remember: "When was it that we saw you?" The cursed and the blessed ask the same question. But while some go their way in life without seeing anything of the suffering that surrounds them, the others come to the aid of those whose neighbors they have become. In other words, it is right indeed that Christians should confess that Jesus is "the Messiah, the Son of the living God" (Matt 16:16)—it is their duty and their responsibility—but "the kingdom prepared . . . since the foundation of the world" (Matt 25:34) will be given only to those, whether Christians or not, in whom Christ recognizes himself, that is, those who are hungry, thirsty, strangers, naked, prisoners, sick; and those who minister to them.

Saint Benedict gives particular attention to these last (RB 36):

> Care of the sick must rank above and before all else so that they may truly be served as Christ, for he said: *I was sick and you visited me* (Matt 25:36), and, *What you did to one of these least brothers, you did for me* (Matt 25:40). Let the sick on their part bear in mind that they are served out of honor for God, and let them not by their excessive demands distress their brothers who serve them. Still, sick brothers must be patiently borne with, because serving them leads to a greater reward. Consequently, the abbot should be extremely careful that they suffer no neglect.

Considering the sick brother or sister as if he or she were Christ comes directly from Matthew 25, explicitly quoted in chapter 36. The remarkable point consists in this, Benedict demands reciprocity. The sick persons will be taken care of in any case; however, they must not forget that it is because they resemble the suffering Christ that they are precisely treated *like Christ*. Let us go further: if the sick are *like Christ*, they must imitate their master who went so far as to not "regard equality with God as something to be exploited" (Phil 2:6). This concept of reciprocity is in full accord with the spirit of the Gospel. And if Jesus exhorts the disciples to go through the narrow door, that is to say, to take seriously the demands of the kingdom, it is because he himself is the door: it is he who opens the way and shows the road he himself has walked. This can be verified in other gospel passages.

★ ★ ★

The story of the cure of the deaf man with a speech impediment in Mark 7:31–37 is as vivid as it is concrete. When listening to it, one has almost the impression of being present at the scene because the language is so earthy: "They *brought* to him *a deaf man who had an impediment in his speech*; and they *begged* him to *lay his hand on him*. . . . He . . . *put his fingers into his ears* and . . . *touched his tongue*. Then, *looking up* to heaven, he *sighed* and said to him *Ephphatha*, that is, *'Be opened.'* And immediately *his ears were opened, his tongue was released*, and he *spoke plainly*."

In Greek, all these nouns and verbs "express an operation of the senses," and, except for "see," call for the genitive. One can ponder over this particularity. A mere mention of it is enough to show that in Greek the verbs relative to the senses enjoy a special status, even grammatically.

It would seem that here grammar has something to do with Christian faith. Since one can always make suppositions, one may think that in order to save humans, God could have acted without mediation. Now everybody knows that precisely, non-mediation is linked with imagination. To lock God into imagination would come down to a denial or, worse, a perversion of God. The wrong thing Adam did after the sin is precisely to *imagine* that God could forget sin; thus, Adam created a God in the likeness and image of humans. "The man and his wife hid themselves from the presence of the Lord God" (Gen 3:8). So for the first time in history—and perhaps it is this question that inaugurates history—God goes searching for humans: "Adam, where are you?" (Gen 3:9).

★ ★ ★

Now, when God began to search for humans, God did not just choose to be close to them. Rather, God wanted to be their neighbor. "And who is my neighbor?" the lawyer asks, wanting to justify himself (Luke 10:29), that is, to justify his question as well as the serious character of his search. By formulating his question in this way, he who had given the right answer, that one must "love one's neighbor as oneself" (10:27), in fact loves only himself: like the sun in the center of the solar system, he considers and situates others in relation to himself. It is precisely by means of the parable of the Good Samaritan (Luke 10:29-37) that Jesus knocks down the lawyer's initial question by asking, "Which of these three, do you think, was a neighbor to the man who fell into the hands of the robbers?" (10:36).

And who is the neighbor of the man who fell into the hands of sinners? Who became the neighbor of this Adam, this word that means *man* in Hebrew? Is it not Jesus, the Son of God? *And the Word became flesh and lived among us* (John 1:14). By the mystery of the Incarnation, God's center ceases to be within God— it is the mystery of the kenosis, to use Paul's language (Phil 2:7). Rather than being simply close to humanity, God becomes the *neighbor* of every human being. In contrast to the priest and levite who *saw and passed by at a safe distance* (Luke 10:31-32), the Samaritan Jesus *was moved with pity*, that is, *was hit in the gut* (10:33) *when he saw* the man stripped, savagely beaten, half-dead. "*I have observed the misery of my people*," God had already said in the past when he *saw* the Hebrews enslaved in Egypt (Exod 3:7).

To see, to be moved with pity, to become flesh, to become a neighbor, these are all verbs that express the merciful tenderness of our God (Luke 1:78) when God sets out to seek humans. "The Son of Man came to seek out and to save the lost" (Luke 19:10), Jesus said at the conclusion of the story of his encounter with Zacheus, thus returning to the well-known themes of the parables in Luke's chapter 15.

★ ★ ★

So Jesus became one of us, taking great care not to make others untouchable and not to became so himself. A proof of this is his encounter with the woman afflicted with a hemorrhage (Mark 5:25-34). She did not dare to openly approach Jesus and enter into conversation with him, a little as if she wanted to take advantage of the power she sensed in him without compromising herself too much. But there is an unshakable trust in her: "If I but touch his clothes, I will be made well" (5:28). Now Jesus forces the one who had approached him in secret to be anonymous no longer. It is as if the healing could be total only on the condition of a reciprocal recognition which Jesus seals with a word, "Daughter, your faith has made you well; go in peace and be healed of your disease" (5:34). Christian faith belongs to the order of relationship. This is one of the principal teachings of this gospel story.

★ ★ ★

"When the Son of Man comes, will he find faith on earth?" (Luke 18:8). This was the initial question, which we may perhaps now be able to answer. It comes within a context strange at first sight; it comes after the passage called *The Parable of the Widow and the Unjust Judge:* words have importance, but this is not the place to discuss the title that should be given to this gospel passage. In reality, in order to understand Jesus' question, one must reread the beginning of the parable: "Then Jesus told them a parable about their need to pray always and not to lose heart" (Luke 18:1). Therefore, if the disciples *do not pray constantly without losing heart,* it is their faith, that is, their faithfulness to the Word of God, which will be imperiled, if not become nonexistent. Since Christian faith is relationship, it is relationship with Christ in an unceasing dialogue (which is called prayer) and relationship with those whose neighbors we have become.

Without a doubt, this point deserves to be taken seriously by Christians. The answer to the question about the end of time must be formulated today in such a way as to insure that faithfulness to Christ may continue through successive generations.

Chapter 7

Vigils and Waiting

Strive for his kingdom.
Luke 12:31

In chapter 11 of the Rule, Saint Benedict regulates the order of Vigils for Sunday. On that day, he writes, "the monks should arise earlier" (RB 11.1). Not for pure asceticism: the lawgiver of the monks reminds them precisely at that point that "there must be moderation in quantity," since moderation is characteristic of Benedictine wisdom. The reason for the earlier rising is simple: the Vigils being longer on Sunday than on the other days of the week, they require more time. To this day, certain monasteries have kept the custom of beginning the day earlier on Sundays and solemnities. Benedict adds another Sunday prescription which is still in use: the "abbot begins the hymn 'We praise you, God.'" Then "he reads from the Gospels while all the monks stand with respect and awe"(RB 11.9). All is planned as if the Sunday Vigils symbolically represented monastic life up to its fullness: after having watched in faith and in prayer through hymns, psalms, and readings, the monastics turn toward the abbot or abbess, who solemnly proclaims the Gospel, the Word of God. It is only after a long wait in the night that Christ, the Light and the Word of God, offers himself to be heard and contemplated. But is not this the symbolic representation and the meaning of every Christian life, whatever its form? Although monastic life is original because of its radical character, it is nothing other than a baptismal life free of any diversion. Christian faith is in fact a waiting for the Lord's coming. It is what constitutes its nobility but also causes one of its main difficulties. As Denis Huerre observes: "To be able to wait patiently as an exercise in *humilitas* as well as a display of courage. We can even find ourselves getting impatient when waiting for someone who actually turns up on time."[1]

It is true that in ordinary life we do not like to wait and we try to wait as little as possible. Waiting rooms do not have more status than the reading material one usually finds there, and everyone has her or his stratagems to cut short or avoid waiting in line. Only the poor use waiting rooms along with those who do not know how to contrive ways of escaping long waits. But those who have power or know-how are the first everywhere. It is true that impatience can be justified if one considers the end to be reached: there is no enjoyment in waiting for one's turn at the window of some administrative office if all one wants is an official stamp on some form. Unless this form is the key that opens the way to unknown horizons. The joy one feels at discovering a foreign country is often beyond any comparison with the tedium of a long wait in an embassy to obtain the precious visa.

★ ★ ★

At this point, it is useful to recall the ancient distinction that John Cassian, one of the fathers of monasticism (5th century), establishes between *the goal* and *the end*. This distinction is both practical and enlightening. To make the difference between the two terms easier to grasp, Abbot Moses asks his visitors, monastics who endure *fasting, the weariness of watches, the assiduity to reading and meditation of the Scriptures, the unending work, the deprivation of everything,* "What is your goal and what is your end,

---

1. Denis Huerre, *Letters to My Brothers and Sisters: Living by the Rule of St. Benedict,* trans. Sylvester Houédard (Collegeville, Minn.: Liturgical Press, 1994) 116.

which drives you to endure all these things so willingly?" And Cassian continues, "And when he insisted on having our answer to this question, we replied that we bore all these things for the sake of the kingdom of heaven.

"On hearing this he said: 'Good! You have spoken well about your end. But before anything else you should know what ought to be our scopos or our goal, by constantly clinging to which we may be able to attain our end.' And when we had in all simplicity confessed our ignorance, he added: 'As I have said, in every art and discipline a certain scopos takes precedence. This is the soul's goal and the mind's constant intention, which cannot be maintained nor the final end of the longed-for fruit arrived at except by an encompassing diligence and perseverance.'"[2] Remembering that the end is farther away than the goal, but that one cannot reach the end without going through the goal, let us quote two examples that Cassian cites among others.

The first one is that of the farmer:

> The farmer who has as his end a secure and comfortable life, thanks to his fruitful lands, pursues his scopos or goal by clearing his field of all the briers and emptying it of every unfruitful weed, and he does not believe that he will achieve his end of peaceful affluence in any other way than as it were by first possessing by toil and hope what he desires to have the actual use of.

Therefore there is no life of plenty for farmers if they do not work in their field day in day out.

The second example is that of warriors:

> It is like those who are accustomed to handling weapons of war: When they want to show off their expertise in this art before a king of this world, they strive to aim their javelins or arrows at some very small targets that have the prizes

2. All quotations of John Cassian in this chapter are taken from "Conference 1: On the Goal of the Monk," in John Cassian, *The Conferences*, trans. Boniface Ramsey (New York: Paulist Press, 1997) 42, 43, 44.

pictured on them. They are certain that other than by the targeted mark they cannot arrive at the end, the sought-after prize which they will possess as soon as they have been able to hit the goal that was set. If perchance it has been removed from their sight, however off-course the vain thrust of the unskilled might be, still they will not think that they have departed from the direction that was set because they have no sure gauge that would show either how accurate the aim was or how bad it was. And, therefore, when they have poured their missiles ineffectually into the airy void, they are unable to judge where they have gone wrong and where they have been led astray, for there is no indication to show them how far they have wandered from the direction, nor can an uncertain eye teach them how they must correct or change their aim.

And Cassian applies to monastic life the difference between the goal and the end

> The end of our profession . . . is the kingdom of God or the kingdom of heaven; but the goal or scopos is purity of heart, without which it is impossible for anyone to reach that end. Fixing our gaze on this goal, then, as on a definite mark, we shall take the most direct route. If our attention should wander somewhat from it we shall at once return to its contemplation, accurately correcting ourselves as by a kind of rule.

★ ★ ★

No one will be surprised when reminded that on the question of the end, Cassian does not invent anything. It is indeed the kingdom of heaven which is the ultimate goal sought by Christ's disciples, as Luke underlines in one of the incisive phrases which are characteristic of his style, "Strive for his kingdom, and these things will be given to you as well" (12:31). In the parallel passage, Matthew makes more explicit Jesus' command by juxtaposing the end and the goal, if we want to use

Cassian's vocabulary: "But strive first for the kingdom of God and his righteousness, and all these things will be given you as well" (Matt 6:33). As always the *first* calls for a *then*. Matthew accepts that the search for the kingdom is primary, without being exclusive. But he especially indicates the means or the goal that allows us to reach the kingdom: to strive for the righteousness of the kingdom, as some manuscripts say, that is, do the will of God as Jesus expresses it in the Sermon on the Mount (Matt 5–7), which one may regard as the charter of the disciple in his quest for the kingdom.

If Cassian has been considered a defender of semi-pelagianism, it is not Luke's fault. The invitation to "strive for the kingdom" that Jesus extends in 12:31 is immediately followed by a surprising statement, "Do not be afraid, little flock, for it is your Father's good pleasure to give you the kingdom" (12:32). How can we reconcile an active and exclusive quest for the kingdom and the gratuitous giving of this same kingdom by the Father? The opposition is only apparent, because the logic here is that of grace: it is because it has pleased the Father to give the kingdom that the disciples must seek it. The search for the kingdom is the human response to God's gratuitous gift, for God is always the initiator.

Therefore, the end we pursue is the kingdom. Let us note in passing that expressions like "to build the kingdom," expressions which are not in the Gospel, contain in themselves a contradiction: far from being our work, the kingdom is a gift from the Father and a gift we must receive and welcome. Thus, in the Gospels several phrases are used to express this welcoming. "The kingdom of God is near," one "enters the kingdom," "you are not far from the kingdom," the one who does not "receive the kingdom like this child." All these are faltering words which attempt to express what concerns the kingdom. In any case, Jesus himself usually speaks of the kingdom in parables, "The Kingdom of God is like. . . ."

Let us emphasize in passing that although the kingdom is a properly eschatological end, it cannot be relegated to a more or less distant future, to the point of being without tie to the present. The difficulty for "those who have wealth to enter the kingdom of God" (Luke 18:24) is not only for tomorrow; the warning Jesus gives is not purely and simply a threat concerning the future entrance into heaven. It is already *today* that "it is easier for a camel to go through the eye of a needle than for someone who is rich to enter the kingdom of God" (Luke 18:25). In the same way, salvation has entered Zacheus' house *today*.

The kingdom is at once "in this age" and "in the age to come" (Luke 18:30). It is both a promise and a present reality: "Blessed are you who are poor for yours is the kingdom of God" (Luke 6:20). Matthew also has the first beatitude in the present tense, thus perfectly agreeing with Luke on this point, "Blessed are the poor in spirit, for theirs is the kingdom of heaven" (Matt 5:3).

"The kingdom of God has come to you" (Luke 11:20) since it is "among you" (Luke 17:21). Nevertheless, Christian faith can be defined as the wait for the coming of the kingdom, *"Marana tha!* Come, Lord Jesus!" (Rev 22:20). But waiting does not mean being passive, even though we must remember that humans are radically unable to bring about the coming of the kingdom. "Thy kingdom come!" This petition expresses the expectation of the human heart and the desire of the human heart to see its destiny fulfilled. We experience this in our own lives: we must often wait for a long time to get the things which are the most meaningful to us. The most beautiful and the most important, those we need in order to live, such as love and friendship, those things come only after a slow germination, and they give themselves to us as pure grace.

In a world where the "right now" rules and where it is more and more possible to obtain instant gratification, Christians are defined as people who, although being genuinely part of this world, are waiting for the coming of a kingdom which is not of this world. Thus, they watch in the night. They watch in faith, sometimes in the night of faith: "The life I now live in the flesh I live by faith in the Son of God, who loved me and gave himself for me" (Gal 2:20). I love to think that even Jesus lived in faith without necessarily always knowing and I love to remind myself of this when I am in the dark.

Although the gift of the kingdom is the end that Christ's disciples wait for, Cassian rightly reminds us that, far from being only a vague aspiration, this ultimate objective of necessity needs a goal which he for his part calls purity of heart: "Having your scopos is purity of heart but your end is eternal life." One can designate the goal by equivalent terms, such as "charity" or "peace," as Cassian does. Whatever the words used, the goal is nothing else than the *sequela Christi*, the walking in the steps of Christ: "If any want to become my followers, let them deny themselves and take up their cross daily and follow me" (Luke 9:23).

By distinguishing *goal* and *end* and by calling *goal* what could appear to be a *means*, Cassian is faithful to both the spirit and the letter of the gospel. Since Christian life is a *way* in which one walks, one cannot regard the following of Christ as the means to arrive at eternal life. When approached by the rich man, whom Luke characterizes as a ruler and who desires to obtain this eternal life (Luke 18:18–23), Jesus reminds him of the commandments. Then in response to the man's insistence, he declares, "There is still one thing lacking. Sell all that you own and distribute the money to the poor, and you will have treasure in heaven; then come, *follow me*" (Luke 18:22). Walking in Jesus' footsteps is thus the sole goal of Christian life, the *ultimate end* of which is entrance into the kingdom which has already begun *today* and which will find its completion in eternity.

"Be alert at all times, praying that you may have the strength to escape all these things that will take place, and to stand before the Son of Man" (Luke 21:36).

Chapter 8

Broken Bread

This is my body, which is given for you.
Luke 22:19

Nothing is more common than bread. It is the staple food, at the time of Jesus as well as in our own time: "Friend, lend me three loaves of bread; for a friend of mine has arrived, and I have nothing to set before him" (Luke 11:5-6).

Bread is what people labor for. Two current phrases are "earn a living" and "put bread on the table."

Bread is the whole life of humans, as we are reminded at each Eucharist at the presentation of the gifts: "Blessed are you, Lord, God of all creation. / Through your goodness we have this bread to offer, / which earth has given and human hands have made." A person from the community of Emmaus, stopping shortly at the monastery, said to the attentive community how much he liked having these words pronounced aloud by the presider so that everybody could hear them. Made by "human hands," the bread we present to God so that it may become "the bread of life" has gone through an incalculable number of hands, from those who sowed the grain, extracted the salt, and drew the water to those which placed the bread on the paten. Those hands were not all pure, far from it. But the product of the work of all those hands will become the bread of eternal life.

> Before he was given up to death,
> a death he freely accepted,
> he took the bread and gave you thanks,
> gave it to his disciples, and said:
> **Take this, all of you, and eat it**
> **this is my body which will be given up for you**
> (Eucharistic Prayer No. 2).

Jesus breaks the bread, thus accomplishing a gesture with which we have become familiar. In many countries, everyone has learned in childhood not to eat from the whole loaf itself but to break it. Bread has to be broken. It is the reason why Jesus breaks the bread. And this broken bread is nothing else than his Body delivered and broken. The Lord's action on the evening of Holy Thursday is inseparable from the torture that he will go through the following day while he is dying on the cross: it is there that his body is broken and given for us.

By breaking the bread on the eve of his death, Jesus performs a prophetic action: he celebrates what he is about to accomplish in his passion and death. And it is impossible to dissociate the institution of the Eucharist, the gift of broken bread, from the royal gift of his life that he makes by suffering the passion and dying on the cross. To participate in the Eucharist is to discern the Body of the Lord given *for us* and to acknowledge that he died *for us and for our salvation*.

Bread must be broken so that it may be shared; otherwise, the symbolism of bread is debased. A meal is not only meant to feed the body. There is nothing sadder than a snack hastily swallowed by someone alone at the corner of a table. A meal is a social act because, thanks to the food taken together, an exchange is created, a relation is established. Thus is born the community of guests because the meal is at the service of communion. Such is our experience, more particularly when we participate in a festive meal.

Benedict was fully conscious of the symbolism of the meal drawn from the Gospels when he prescribes that a monastic guilty of a serious fault be excluded from the common table: "Let him take his food alone in an amount and at a time the abbot considers appropriate for him. He should not be blessed by anyone passing by, nor should the food that is given him be blessed" (RB 25.5-6). Even today the meal in a monastic community has a liturgical tonality. Although many ancient customs have been fortunately abandoned, that of going in procession through the cloister to the refectory is still customary in many monasteries. Thus, there is a bond established between the meal which is about to be taken and the Eucharist in which one has participated. The same seriousness characterizes both moments. The food is blessed, a sign that it is a gift from God to be shared.

If at present bread is not shared with such great numbers of women and men who are starving, suffer malnutrition, or lack the basic things necessary for a decent and dignified life, it is not because God abandons humans; rather, it is because humans abandon humans, because humans refuse to share the bread that should be available to all. I know well that economic problems are extremely complex and cannot be solved either by beautiful words or good intentions. Nevertheless, the command of Jesus to his disciples, "You give them something to eat" (Luke 9:13) deserves to be heard.

Of course, Jesus' command can be understood in a wide sense. Many women and men, who are not necessarily far away from us, are hungry for justice, peace, respect for their rights and their faith; others are hungry for a fate other than waiting for death. In any case, let us note that as long as there is hunger, there is hope because there is still the desire for life. Those who are no longer hungry for anything are those who are the most to be pitied. Certain images are shattering, like that of the child who refuses the glass of water offered because he or she no longer has the strength to take it and probably no longer has the desire to live.

We know that in John's Gospel there is no account of the institution of the Eucharist; it is replaced by the account of the washing of the feet (John 13:1-17). One can be surprised, even scandalized as was Peter, "Lord, are you going to wash my feet?" In any case, Jesus wants to make sure that the action he just accomplished is properly understood by the disciples, "Do you know what I have done to you?" And Jesus is so unsure of the understanding of the disciples that without waiting for their answer, he explains the meaning of the washing of the feet: "If I, your Lord and Teacher, have washed your feet, you also ought to wash one another's feet. For I have set you an example, that you also should do as I have done to you" (John 13:14-15).

Jesus' action is altogether extraordinary: he, the Lord and Teacher (John 13:14), the Word from the beginning (John 1:1), here he is at the feet of his disciples. Here is the Son of God looking up at humans from below, in the posture of a slave. This leads Aelred of Rievaulx to exhort his reader: "Think of the majesty of the one who washes and wipes these men's feet, of his forbearance when he comes to touch the traitor's feet with his sacred hands. Meditate on the whole scene, wait for him, and . . . go and present your feet for him to wash because anyone who will not have been cleansed by him will have no part with him."[1]

> [He] who, though he was in the form of God
>> did not regard equality with God
>> as something to be exploited,
> but emptied himself,
>> taking the form of a slave . . .
>> he humbled himself
>> and became obedient to the point of death—
>> even death on a cross (Phil 2:6-8).

Although of very different literary genres, the hymn in the Letter to the Philippians and the scene of the washing of the

---

1. Aelred of Rievaulx, *La vie de recluse[et] La prière pastorale*, trans. Charles Dumont, Sources chrétiennes 76 (Paris: Cerf, 1961) 131–133, quoted by Philippe Baud, *La ruche de Cîteaux: les plus belles pages des premiers Pères cisterciens*, Epiphanie: tradition monastique (Paris: Cerf, 1997) 146.

feet express, in fact, the same theological and spiritual model, that of the servant who gives his or her life out of love: "I am among you as one who serves" (Luke 22:27).

One does not take part in the Eucharist only to restore one's strength but to make a commitment. Sharing in the Body and Blood of the Lord is equivalent to consenting to wash the feet of our fellow humans, brothers and sisters, placing ourselves at their service, sharing with them the bread, fruit of the earth and the work of all humans.

★ ★ ★

There is bread only if it is broken.

There is bread only if it is shared.

There is bread only to satisfy hunger. But we must add that this satisfaction is just temporary. Today we are eating, but tomorrow we shall be hungry again. Bread is for today's hunger. It is what we daily ask from God when we say the Our Father. *Give us this day our daily bread.*

The good bread is not the one we reserve for later, in imitation of the Hebrew people who in their travels across the desert, in spite of their God's orders, wanted to hoard manna today for fear of want tomorrow. It is so human to fear to be without. In fact the only good bread is that which allows us to continue on our way. On the way a new hunger will develop, and we will have to satisfy it without having any assurance that there will be bread on the day following. One monk of Tamié tells us: "The first time I went to visit the brothers at Tibhirine was a December evening. It was raining, it was cold, snow was in the offing. In a word, it was sad. . . . But hardly had I arrived in that house, their house, poor and warm at the same time, I heard a conviction taking shape in the bottom of my heart: I felt that these men were the true monks of today. Everything in their life was stamped with the seal of precarity."[2]

2. Philippe Hémon, Frère, "C'étaient mes frères, c'étaient des moines . . .," in *Sept vies pour Dieu et l'Algérie*, ed. Bruno Chenu (Paris: Bayard, 1996).

Without a doubt, we forget all too often in our day that precarity, another name for poverty, is a given in Christian living. Every authentic Christian life is characterized by a certain lack of security as to the morrow. Nothing surprising here since Christians are the disciples of the Son of Man, who had no place to rest his head.

Jesus gives himself to us in the Eucharist, "Take and eat" he says. It is a command that must be reiterated without ceasing. Why? Because by eating this bread, we hollow out in us an ever increasing hunger for God.

Chapter 9

Passion

Here is the man.
John 19:5

Sometimes evidence needs to be underlined: the accounts of the passion of Christ occupy a very important place in our Gospels, out of proportion with the totality of the evangelical corpus. For instance, the passion narrative constitutes one fifth of Mark's Gospel. It is a large amount when one considers Jesus' life from his birth to his death, and it is an even larger amount if one considers the only period which Mark describes, the period that extends from John the Baptist's preaching (Mark 1:2-8) to the brief scene of the open tomb (Mark 16:1-8). And some witty exegetes—some of these do exist!—are justified in characterizing Mark's Gospel as a passion narrative preceded by a long introduction. This clever remark expresses an essential truth: there is no Gospel without proclamation of the Cross.

Our prevalent psychology as well as our spontaneous tendencies incline us to emphasize joy rather than sadness, success rather than failure. Without minimizing the Good News of the Resurrection, the early Christian communities readily understood that it was impossible to enter into the mystery of the Son of God while ignoring his suffering and death. One might think that with the passage of time, the relation would be reversed: the Cross would be relegated to the background. This did not happen since in John's Gospel, the last of the four Gospels to be written, Jesus' death coincides very exactly with the hour of his glorification. John notes that "as yet there was no Spirit, because Jesus was not yet glorified" (John 7:39). As an echo to this statement, we have the brief announcement of Jesus' death, "he gave up his spirit" (John 19:30). It is Jesus' death, that is, his glorification, which makes possible the gift of the Spirit.

A short time before suffering his passion, Jesus had told the Jews, "When you have lifted up the Son of Man, then you will realize that I am he" (John 8:28). Thus, the crucifixion of the Son of Man is an elevation in the two meanings of the word: the standing cross is the sign that the Son of Man is *above everything*, as in the past the bronze serpent in the desert (John 3:14; see Num 21:4-9). No sign has been left to us other than the cross: only the cross signifies for us that Jesus is the Son of the Father because we arrive at faith in the Resurrection only through the event of the Cross.

The statement is paradoxical: how can a disfigured face let a reflection of God's glory show through? And yet, including on the cross, and perhaps especially on the cross, Jesus is "the image of the invisible God" (Col 1:15). Faced with this tortured human being, we must recognize, without being able to explain how, that God resembles someone kneeling in order to serve his disciples (John 13:4-5), someone in the throes of agony, dying like a common criminal. Although their purposes are vastly different, Mark and John are in agreement on this point.

It is well known that the plan of the Second Gospel revolves around a question, "Who then is this?" (Mark 4:41). Answers are given as the gospel sequence unfolds. The first part culminates with Peter's confession, true but significantly incomplete, "You are the Messiah" (Mark 8:29). We must pursue our course although an ambiguity remains: What sort of messiah is Jesus? The denouement of the action is reached only at the centurion's profession of faith, "Truly this man was God's Son" (Mark 15:39). One must be fully aware of the importance of the moment in which these words are spoken: it is because the centurion "saw the way that he breathed his last" that he (the centurion) can proclaim the identity of Jesus. In other words, according to Mark's way of seeing, Jesus can be recognized only in the contemplation of the Cross. Only the Cross allows us to recognize in this human being the one who has been proclaimed the beloved Son at the scene of the baptism, which is the first christological revelation in the Gospel (Mark 1:11). The Cross upends time: before the event on Golgotha, that is to say, during the time of the "beginning of the good news" (Mark 1:1), it belongs to the Father to say who Jesus is (some demons also proclaimed Jesus' identity [Mark 1:24; 5:7]). In contrast, from now on it is possible for all humans, through the pagan centurion's voice, to confess their faith in Jesus. Unique Event, only the Cross allows for the birth of the paschal kerygma: "He has been raised; he is not here" (Mark 16:6).

According to John's vision of things, God is the All-Other· "No one has ever seen God" (John 1:18). And yet, through Jesus, God became our neighbor, one of us, a human being among human beings: "It is God the only Son, who is close to the Father's heart, who has made him known" (John 1:18). Perhaps we can resolve the paradox by looking at Pilate, who at the moment of presenting to the crowd a Jesus wearing a purple robe and a crown of thorns (John 19:1-5), utters these simple words, *Ecce homo* ("Here is the man," John 19:5).

Here is the man who was just delivered to the soldiers' cruelty, flogged and struck on the face (John 19:3). *Here is the man*, as he appears to the crowd, who shouts "Crucify him! Crucify him!" (John 19:6). *Here is the man*, says Pilate, never suspecting how accurately he speaks. Here is the face of injured humanity. The disfigured Jesus is the very image of our sisters and brothers in humanity.

Here he is, resembling all the tortured of the earth, all the victims of war, catastrophe, attack, accident, disease. Jesus, crowned, ridiculed, killed, is one with our humanity, as Aelred of Rievaulx underscores: "Yes, he is really a human being. Who would doubt it? The marks of the whip are here as a proof, the livid wounds and the foulness of the spittle. At last, Satan, understand that this is a human being."[1]

We often ask about—with reason but with a sort of bitter surprise—what we call the problem of evil. How can God allow so much suffering on our earth, the suffering of children who are victims of human perversity, the suffering of women and men unjustly accused or finding life meaningless, the suffering of parents losing a child, the suffering of those who go from failure to failure, the suffering of those who are betrayed? The list could go on and on, and everyone could name the suffering she or he endures or the one whose suffering she or he is powerless to alleviate.

Everyone knows that there is no satisfying answer to the problem of evil. We must speak of suffering with extreme reserve if we must speak about it at all. On this subject, a remark by Cardinal Veuillot, the archbishop of Paris, comes back to me. In February 1968, as he was dying in the hospital, he confided to his close coworkers: "We have made beautiful discourses on suffering. I myself have spoken of it with fervor. Tell the priests to say nothing about it. We do not know what it is. I have been weeping over the whole thing."

Those who deal with people in pain know well that the words they pronounce are not what is important. As disciples of Christ, all we can do is to say in faith that Jesus, the Son of God, has shared our condition to the point of assuming its suffering. He even underwent evil and violence unjustly since he, the innocent, was put to death as an evildoer. Jesus mistreated and disfigured is for us the sign that no human situation, painful as it may be, is foreign to God. We know that Jesus goes before us on the Way of the Cross.

Through this disfigured Jesus, we sense what our God is for us: a God who certainly does not spare us the vicissitudes of the

1. Philippe Baud, *La ruche de Cîteaux: les plus belles pages des premiers Pères cisterciens*, Epiphanie: tradition monastique (Paris: Cerf, 1997) 148.

human condition, but a God who becomes our neighbor in Jesus.[2] If, as we have said, the disfigured Jesus is the very image of our humanity, this same disfigured Jesus is at the same time "the image of the invisible God" (Col 1:15), a God who loves so much that he really makes his own the sufferings of humanity.

It is good to remember that the word passion does not mean only suffering. It designates also a strong and powerful love. The passion of Jesus is his infinite love as much as his suffering. Let us understand clearly: if it is "through his sufferings that we are healed," it is not suffering per se which is saving. Suffering is only the expression of a total love, of a passion that goes "to the bitter end." And everyone knows that, mysteriously, love is always connected with suffering.

★ ★ ★

In a homily given on September 14, 1993, on the feast of the Holy Cross, brother Christian de Chergé, prior of the Atlas, wrote, "We shall remember this primary message for anyone who wants to speak of the cross: we must be there, in silence, like Mary, with arms extended in order to offer everything, joys and sufferings intermingled, in order to welcome everything, sword and glory together. All this makes the cross our place of encounter with Jesus. *Cruci fac nos consortes* (make us sharers of the cross). It is the motto of Latroun."[3]

For, if the cross leads us to contemplation, it is because it is for us, as it was for Jesus, a mystery of interior life; it it is a mystery of interior life before being this sign on our chests or our altars. The cross is not a symbol whose glory would depend upon our boldness to brandish it in all circumstances. For humans, dignity consists in being a cross, as Saint Bernard notes,[4] for humans have the shape of a cross; they are cruciform: "Let

2. See above, chapter 6, p. 26.

3. Latroun: a Cistercian abbey situated between Tel-Aviv and Jerusalem, close to a possible site of the gospel story of the disciples of Emmaus.

4. Bernard of Clairvaux, fourth Sermon on the Vigil of the Nativity.

them extend their hands," Bernard says, "and this becomes even more evident. There their glory begins. There the glorious cross begins. From creation, humans are made in the image of God."[5]

The stress the Gospels place on the Passion, the suffering and the death of Jesus on the cross, has obviously an eminently pastoral purpose. The Passion concerns all humans as we have said. And who among us can pretend not to carry her or his cross? What is the connection between Jesus' cross and our own crosses? The passion narratives point us in the right direction. Jesus lived the passion that led him to death, but mysteriously as well as ineluctably, the Resurrection was already at work within the Passion. The latter was the soil from which Life burst forth: "Was it not necessary that the Messiah should suffer these things and then enter into his glory?" (Luke 24:26).

I do not want to yield to the facility of beautiful discourses. So in order to end this meditation, I could not do any better than offer a consoling thought, provided that it is understood in its noble sense. "A stumbling block to Jews and foolishness to Gentiles" (1 Cor 1:23), the sign of the cross, what we trace on ourselves, has become the sign of our faith in the Triune God. Which means the event of the cross was necessary for God to reveal fully what God is: Father, Son, and Holy Spirit.

5. Bruno Chenu, *Sept vies pour Dieu et l'Algérie* (Paris: Bayard, 1996).

Chapter 10

Signs and Humility

You cannot interpret the signs of the times.
Matt 16:3

This took place a few years ago. A group of us had arrived one evening at the foot of Mount Sinai. The following morning we had gotten up very early in order to reach the summit of the mountain before sunrise. Once at the top, we patiently waited for the sun to rise. It was very cold. A quasi-religious silence prevailed and was troubled only by the click of our cameras. And little by little, from our vantage point dominating all the surrounding mountains, we saw the sun slowly emerge. The spectacle was the more impressive because we were in the middle of a desert and the more moving because we were in a holy place: it is on Sinai, also called Horeb in the Bible, that tradition places both the Covenant that God concluded with Moses and the gift of the Law.

When we went down, I was still filled with wonder at the vision I had contemplated and I was trying to arouse the same enthusiasm in my companions. Then one of my friends, a priest from Costa Rica said to me, "You know, after all, in my country it is the same sun!" This remark first left me dumbfounded, then it made me smile, and finally I found it quite pertinent. It is true: the sun is the same everywhere and God is the same everywhere. There is no need to see a sunrise on Sinai in order to meet God.

I remember this anecdote each time I happen to hear or read the biblical passage depicting the encounter between God and the prophet Elijah, which precisely took place on Horeb (1 Kgs 19:9-18):

> Now there was a great wind, so strong that it was splitting mountains and breaking rocks in pieces before the LORD, but the LORD was not in the wind; and after the wind an earthquake, but the LORD was not in the earthquake; and after the earthquake a fire, but the LORD was not in the fire; and after the fire, a sound of sheer silence. When Elijah heard it, he wrapped his face in his mantle and went out and stood at the entrance of the cave. Then there came a voice to him that said, "What are you doing here, Elijah?" He answered, "I have been very zealous for the LORD, the God of hosts; for the Israelites have forsaken your covenant, thrown down your altars, and killed your prophets with the sword. I alone am left, and they are seeking my life, to take it away" (1 Kgs 19:11-14).[1]

While the prophet Elijah has imagined a God Sabaoth, that is, a God of armies, a God mastering cosmic forces such as the wind and the fire, here he is led to understand that God passes by in sheer silence; God reveals the divine self in what is almost nothing: silence, humility, and prayer. I find this text of the encounter of Elijah with God extraordinary. What God does is send us back to the ordinary and the banality of our life. The sun can well take different shapes and colors according to the places from where it is viewed and from which we let it bathe us in light. The action of the sun, through the solar wind, in an aurora borealis is vastly different from its direct action at midday in the tropics. Nevertheless the sun is always the sun. Created in the image of God, who is God. It is not necessary to have an uncommon spiritual experience in order to encounter God no

---

1. The author has used the translation of the Jerusalem Bible, slightly modified.

more than it is necessary to climb Thabor, where tradition places the transfiguration, in order to experience the living Christ. Wherever one prays is a holy land: "The cell is a holy land and a holy place; it is there that the Lord and his servant often speak together face to face, as one speaks to a friend (Exod 33:11)."[2]

We often imagine that God speaks to us only in extraordinary events. The Gospels show rather that faith has to be lived in dailiness, in humility, even in a certain monotonousness.

When Jesus cures the sick, it is to invite them to "go home," that is, to go inside themselves so that opposite inner forces that fought within them may be reconciled and they may cease to be divided human beings. Thus, the possessed person of Gerasa, whom the people find "sitting there, clothed and in his right mind, the very man who had had the legion" (Mark 5:15). To get dressed, to be able to sit, to be in possession of one's psychological and intellectual faculties are all properly human characteristics. Jesus even goes so far as not to allow the former demoniac to follow him, in spite of his desire. It will be enough for him to "go home to [his] friends and tell them how much the Lord has done for [him]" (Mark 5:19). Nothing extraordinary in this new life that now begins for the one Jesus has made whole by reintegrating into humankind the one who once bruised himself with stones and was impossible to restrain (Mark 5:3-5).

★ ★ ★

In view of the ordinariness of this new life, why do the Synoptics report for us the transfiguration of Jesus (Mark 9:2-10)? Does not this scene suggest to us that Jesus himself had reached the apex of his encounter with God on the mountain, in a way both unique and extraordinary? According to Mark's Gospel, Jesus had just announced to his disciples for the first time his

2. William of Saint-Thierry, *Lettre aux fères du Mont-Dieu: lettre d'or*, trans. Jean Déchanet, Sources chrétiennes 223 (Paris: Cerf, 1975), paragraph 35.

passion, his death, and his resurrection (Mark 8:31–33). Peter had just recognized in Jesus the Messiah (Mark 8:29). Now Jesus must act in such a way that his disciples may understand what sort of messiah he is. Not a victorious king imposing himself by his power, but a disconcerting messiah who goes to glory through the cross: "Then he began to teach them that the Son of Man must undergo great suffering, and be rejected by the elders, the chief priests, and the scribes, and be killed, and after three days rise again" (Mark 8:31). The disciples are stunned, Peter in particular. He cannot accept that such a fate be reserved for the one he just has confessed to be the Messiah. So he proceeds to "rebuke" Jesus. He is called *Satan* in these words: "Get behind me, Satan! For you are setting your mind not on divine things but on human things" (Mark 8:33). This is a call to humility addressed to Peter and to disciples of all times: it is possible to oppose God even when one has just said good things about God.

Jesus then explains to the crowd as well as to his disciples that to follow him, one has to imitate him: "If any want to become my followers, let them deny themselves and take their cross and follow me. For those who want to save their life will lose it, and those who lose their life for my sake, and for the sake of the gospel, will save it" (Mark 8:34–35). Thus, the cross of Christ must be freely accepted by those who want to be his disciples. And in any case, "there are some standing here who will not taste death until they see that the kingdom of God has come with power" (Mark 9:1).

As a sort of illustration of this statement, the scene of the Transfiguration comes at this point; Peter, James, and John, the followers of Jesus from the beginning to Gethsemane, were the privileged witnesses of this apocalyptic scene.[3] Its apex occurs at the moment when, as it did at the baptism, the voice from the cloud is heard, "This is my Son, the Beloved; listen to him!" (Mark 9:7). From this viewpoint, one may regard the Transfiguration as *a paschal sign* given to the three disciples. Just after Jesus

---

3. In Greek, *apocalypse* means *unveiling, revelation.*

announced his passion, his death, and his resurrection, *he was transfigured before them* (Mark 9:2), thus allowing the disciples to contemplate his truest and deepest identity, that of Son of God from all eternity. It was like a warning, given to Peter, James, and John, who will witness his battle in Gethsemane (Mark 14:32-42), that his disfigurement will be the passage to the definitive transfiguration. Did the disciples understand the sign? Nothing is less sure since two more times will Jesus have to foretell his death and his resurrection (Mark 9:30-32; 10:32-34). The Gethsemane story suggests that the three disciples have remained blind to the mystery of Jesus: "Simon, are you asleep? Could you not keep awake one hour? Keep awake and pray that you may not come into the time of trial" (Mark 14:37-38).

★ ★ ★

The truth is that before *interpreting* a sign, one must *see* it. When the Pharisees and the Sadducees ask for a sign (Matt 16:1-4), Jesus begins by taking an example that speaks to all since it is the topic that feeds most ordinary conversations: What will tomorrow's weather be like? Already at the time of Jesus, everybody knew that a red morning sky announces wind and storm, whereas an evening red sky promises fair weather. This is precisely the reproach Jesus addresses to those who know how to decipher the signs of the weather while being unable to read the signs of the times, "You know how to interpret the appearance of the sky, but you cannot interpret the signs of the times. An evil and adulterous generation asks for a sign, but no sign will be given to it except the sign of Jonah."

★ ★ ★

Let us note the evolution that the sign has undergone in our Gospels. In the oldest, Mark's, the sign is considered in a completely negative way:

> The Pharisees came and began to argue with him, asking
> him for a sign from heaven, to test him. And he sighed deeply

in his spirit and said, "Why does this generation ask for a sign? Truly I tell you, no sign will be given to this genera-tion" (Mark 8:11-13).

If one takes the context of this episode into account, one cannot miss the irony of the situation. Through two multiplica-tions of loaves (Mark 6:30-44; 8:1-10), Jesus just renewed the miracle of the manna in the desert, described as "bread from heaven" (Exod 16:4). Now the Pharisees ask him precisely for "a sign from heaven," which he has just performed. In any case, according to Mark's Gospel, the miracle is self-sufficient: it needs to be interpreted in faith without having to be explained.

In Matthew and Luke, the same reticence regarding the sign is noticeable, although it is somewhat tempered by the gift of the sign of Jonah (Matt 16:4; Luke 11:29), even though the two evangelists do not give the same meaning to that sign. On the other hand, in John's Gospel, the sign is strongly rehabilitated to such an extent that it is customary to name the first part of St. John's work "The Book of Signs." And in the conclusion of the Gospel, the author is careful to remark that "Jesus did many other signs in the presence of his disciples which are not writ-ten in this book" (John 20:29-30).

★ ★ ★

These different ways of understanding the sign at the very center of the Gospels shows well how ambiguous the sign can be. These ways of understanding remain ambiguous, and I be-lieve that for us signs are as difficult to interpret as they were in Jesus' time. Of course, it is easy for us to pooh-pooh the dis-ciples, who did not understand the sign of the bread because of the hardness of their hearts (Mark 8:14-21). But are we better than they in understanding the mystery of Jesus (Mark 8:17-18)?

Something can guide us to the right way when it is a ques-tion of reading the signs of the times. When Jesus reproaches his hearers, whether disciples or opponents, he often attributes their inability to discern the signs to the bad disposition of their hearts. Thus in Mark, "Are your hearts hardened?" (Mark 8:17) or in Matthew, "An evil and adulterous generation asks for a sign" (Matt 16:4). In other words, only the humble of heart are able to see and read the signs that God performs for them.

When the archangel Gabriel announces John's birth to him (Luke 1:5-25), Zechariah asks a question which is a demand: "How will I know that it is so?" (Luke 1:18). Rather than *trusting* the divine messenger, he wants *to know*. Faith and knowledge are two realities that ill agree with one another when they compete. If Zechariah is reduced to silence, it is because he *"did not believe [the] words, which will be fulfilled in their time"* (Luke 1:20). When Gabriel announces the birth of Jesus to Mary, she asks a question which is of the order of *faith*, "How can this be?" (Luke 1:34). Without trying *to know*, she seeks *to understand*. Her humility guides her behavior. She does not seek to fathom the mystery of God, but to comply with it. One can perceive a sign only in the humility of faith. Thus, William of Saint-Thierry comments: "The believer's humility is the surest mark of the Lord's sheep, which will be placed at God's right hand; conversely the proud question of whoever refuses to believe is the mark of the goat, which will be placed at God's left."[4]

It is in that same perspective that Thomas Merton, author of *La nuit privée d'étoiles*,[5] writes at the beginning of his book *The Sign of Jonas:*

> The sign Jesus promised to the generation that did not understand Him was the "sign of Jonas the prophet"—that is, the sign of His own resurrection. The life of every monk, of every priest, of every Christian is signed with the sign of Jonas, because we all live by the power of Christ's Resurrection. But I feel that my own life is especially sealed with this great sign, which baptism and monastic profession and

---

4. William of Saint-Thierry, *Le miroir de la foi*, trans. Jean Déchanet, Sources chrétiennes 301 (Paris: Cerf, 1982) 80–81.

5. Thomas Merton, *La nuit privée d'étoiles*, coll. "Livre de Vie 2-3" (Paris: Albin Michel, 1951).

priestly ordination have burned into the roots of my being, because like Jonas himself I find myself traveling toward my destiny in the belly of a paradox.[6]

★ ★ ★

Humility is without a doubt the spiritual attitude most difficult to maintain because it risks to founder on two opposed reefs. A monastic prayer taken from one or the other of the "little hours"[7] rightly mentions them. We ask God to grant us the true humility which is "neither pride nor humiliation." From this point of view, I confess that I was very impressed for a long time by this word of La Rochefoucauld, "It is possible to desire humility through pride." It seemed to me that such a statement discredited every form of humility since one could immediately suspect its motivations. Then one day, I understood that the humility La Rochefoucauld was speaking of was not humility. What we desire through pride is pride because it is purity of heart that determines the quality of our acts: "The things that come out are what defile" (Mark 7:15). Similarly, to give others the impression or the feeling that we are nothing is not a matter of humility but of unwholesome self-humiliation. In any case, if we willingly speak of "true humility," it is probably because there exists a false one which is never very far. True humility causes us to walk along a ridge, and we must continually verify the rightness of our attitude.

When I started to be familiar with the Rule, I was surprised by the importance Benedict gives to humility. And in the lengthy chapter he devotes to it, he proposes twelve steps, which shows that it takes a long time to reach the summit. He concludes (RB 7.67-70):

---

6. Thomas Merton, *The Sign of Jonas* (New York: Harcourt, Brace and Company, 1953) 11.

7. The little hours are the offices at approximately mid-morning, at noon, and at approximately mid-afternoon.

Now, therefore, after ascending all these steps of humility, the monk will quickly arrive at that *perfect love* of God which *casts out fear* (1 John 4:18). Through this love, all that he once performed with dread, he will now begin to observe without effort, as though naturally, from habit, no longer out of fear of hell, but out of love for Christ, good habit and delight in virtue. All this the Lord will by the holy Spirit graciously manifest in his workman now cleansed of vices and sins.

These lines are surprising. Benedict explains to us that it is humility which makes us pass from a religion of fear to the love of God and Christ. What secret properties does this virtue possess that makes it the cause of such a transformation?

I believe that humility opens the eyes of the heart. It makes us capable of seeing what is not immediately perceptible to the eye. As a consequence, only those who live in the humility of faith can read the signs of the resurrection of Christ in our world as well as in their own lives, as Thomas Merton says. Like the Virgin Mary standing at the foot of the cross (John 19:25–27). It is a long apprenticeship that leads us from the fear of hell to the gratuitous love of the Father, the Son, and the Holy Spirit. In fact, the three persons of the Trinity are named in the conclusion of chapter 7, which deals with humility. It is the one single time the Rule names the three Persons together.[8] Is not this the sign that Benedict regards humility as the chief virtue of the monastic? And therefore of the Christian?

8. The Holy Spirit is named two other times in the Rule, in the Prologue, 11, and in chapter 49.6.

Chapter 11

Conversion

Repent and believe in the good news.
Mark 1:15

When Jesus encounters the man blind from birth, the disciples immediately ask him, "Rabbi, who sinned, this man or his parents, that he was born blind?" (John 9:1-2). All the notes at the bottom of the pages of our Bibles accurately explain that, according to the conception of that time, people established a connection between sin and infirmities, the former being the cause of the latter. People wanted to know whether the guilt rested with the parents or the child. Hence the disciples' question.

Such a conception of course makes us smile. We think ourselves well beyond a reasoning as simplistic as it is grim. However, a mere look around us shows us that in the imagination, whether collective of individual, misfortune is closely linked with culpability. At bottom, misfortune is the ransom to pay for faults one has committed. I am always surprised to see how strenuously we hunt for the culprits of whom our contemporary society is both the cause and the victim. If a tree falls during a storm and kills some people, a complaint is lodged against X for involuntary homicide. As if there had to be at any cost someone responsible for the fall of a tree. It is a fact that projecting a collective culpability onto an individual reassures everybody, except, of course, the so-called guilty person. I believe we are not far from the attitude of Jesus' contemporaries who insisted on finding someone responsible for the collapse of the tower of Siloam: As to "those eighteen who were killed when the tower of Siloam fell on them—do you think that they were worse offenders than all the others living in Jerusalem? No, I tell you; but unless you repent, you will all perish just as they did" (Luke 13:4-5).

Jesus' word is strange. On the one hand, it frees us from every false guilt and takes us away from the caricatural image of a vengeful God. On the other hand, it plunges us into as great a peril, "Unless you repent, you will all perish just as they did." One feels Jesus is indulging in a sort of ultimatum: it is conversion or death.

However, it is true, there is no other alternative. To undergo conversion is really a question of life and death. In these conditions, how are we to understand the call to conversion? Is it to pile penance on top of penance, sacrifice on top of sacrifice? There is some of this in conversion. But we must recognize that the modern mentality does not prepare us for this sort of exercise. Only in some monasteries is fasting still in force. Through the perpetual abstinence from meat and a certain sobriety in the use of other foods according to Saint Benedict's advice, monastics want to wean themselves from all that could enslave them and to remember that they depend on God from whom they receive their food.[1] Even though, as older monastics themselves say without manifesting any regret, fasting today is considerably mitigated, I believe that I never truly fasted before my stay in the monastery. In that regard, Ash Wednesday is particularly outstanding. On that day, when the menu is restricted to bread and water in some monasteries, "each one is to receive a book from the library, and is to read the whole of it straight through" (RB 48.15). Thus the monastics are reminded that "one does

---

1. See, Michel Quesnel, *L'éternité qui m'est offerte* (Paris: Desclée de Brouwer, 1998) 101–102.

not live by bread alone, but by every word that comes from the mouth of God" (Matt 4:4).

Saint Benedict, who knows well the human heart, knows that the community ascesis monastics practice could lead them to believe that they derive their strength from their own selves, which would fill their hearts with pride. So he gives this recommendation: "During these days, we will add to the usual measure of our service something by way of private prayer and abstinence from food and drink, so that each of us will have something above the assigned measure to offer God of his own will *with the joy of the Holy Spirit* (1 Thess 1:6). In other words, let each one deny himself some food, drink, sleep, needless talking and idle jesting, and look forward to holy Easter with joy and spiritual longing" (RB 49.5-7).

But here again, wisdom suggests to Benedict to give a warning against every form of pride: "Everyone should, however, make known to the abbot what he intends to do, since it ought to be done with his prayer and approval. Whatever is undertaken without the permission of the spiritual father will be reckoned as presumption and vainglory, not deserving a reward. Therefore, everything must be done with the abbot's approval" (RB 49.8-10).

* * *

I believe that in this present time, one cannot say too much about how important ascesis is in Christian life, principally through alms, prayer, and fasting (Matt 6:1-18). It is this gospel passage—truncated, it is true, for a reason that I have been seeking in vain—which reminds us at the beginning of every Lent. This being said, all these practices, particularly fasting, are only means to help us attain the true goal of conversion. Still more precisely, to use Cassian's vocabulary,[2] I believe that *the end* of conversion is to discover the true face of God, the one that Jesus reveals to us, to counteract our tendency to create a God in our

2. See chapter 7, p. 34.

image and likeness. But we reach this *end* only by passing through *goals*. What is at stake is to have the experience of the encounter with God, especially through prayer, in order for us *to return* to God (it is the first meaning of the verb to *be converted*). Conversion is achieved by doing God's will, that is to say, by living in conformity with his word. It is in this perspective that we purify our hearts through fasting and that we open ourselves to others through almsgiving. On this subject, I like Michel Quesnel's warning: "replacing fasting by almsgiving is somehow perverse. The mixture serves neither the one nor the other, because fasting and almsgiving have their own separate value."[3]

★ ★ ★

Since conversion is a return to the God of Jesus Christ, why not look for God's face in the First Testament, particularly in the scene, both famous and often commented upon, of the Burning Bush (Exod 3:1-15)? God is like a burning bush which burns without being consumed. What does this image mean if not that God is the All-Other, the God before whom we must take off our sandals, the God whom we cannot approach by our mere humanity unless it is God who calls us first to the meeting? And now the All-Other is also the One who even before revealing God's name to Moses, adds those stunning words: "*I have observed* the misery of my people who are in Egypt; *I have heard* their cry on account of their taskmasters. Indeed *I know* their sufferings, and *I have come down* to deliver them from the Egyptians. . . ." (Exod 3:7-8).

The God who is Other is also the God who intervenes in favor of humans and grants them salvation. However, God does not permit the divine self to be imprisoned in one formula. So it is a response full of mystery that is given to Moses, who wants to know God's name:

3. Ibid., 102.

If I come to the Israelites and say to them "the God of your ancestors has sent me to you," and they ask me, "what is his name?" what shall I say to them? God said to Moses, "I AM WHO I AM" (Exod 3:13-14).

God's name is more a program than a definition. Without satisfying Moses' curiosity, the formula by which God reveals the divine identity opens a future: God is the one who will intervene in the history of God's people.

God is still at work in our world. It is true that, in a certain climate of despair, it is often difficult to discern God's presence. As Augustine Guillerand writes: "Of course the appearances are disconcerting. The world is full of evil and hatred. How can we see love in manifestations so opposed to it? We do not see it, we believe in it. To believe is to see in God's light; it is to trust in God who has said: 'Your bodily eyes, your reason see the evil. But these views are superficial. The bottom of everything is love; believe me who declare it to you.' We see that faith exacts a costly sacrifice; but we also see that it gives us a security and a peace which could be called infinite since they rest on the very word of God. We have the deep secret of Christian tranquillity in the midst of the worst events. The events are passing; God's word is eternal."[4]

★ ★ ★

Dom Augustine opportunely reminds us of the importance of God's word. There is no possible conversion if beforehand there is no word that provokes it: *fides ex auditu* (faith comes from hearing): "But how are they to call on one in whom they have not believed? And how are they to believe in one whom they have never heard? And how are they to hear without someone to proclaim him? And how are they to proclaim him unless they are sent. . . ? So faith comes from what is heard, and what is heard comes from the word of Christ" (Rom

4. Augustin Guillerand, *Voix cartusienne* (Saint-Maur: Parole et Silence, 2001) 42.

10:14–17). An echo to these questions posed by Paul is found in the first word of Jesus in Mark's Gospel: "The time is fulfilled, and the kingdom of God has come near; repent, and believe in the good news" (Mark 1:14–15). Thus, a connection is established between the Word, that is the Gospel, and conversion. *To believe* the Gospel, in other words, to be faithful to the word of Christ, is to initiate a process of conversion.

It is therefore understandable why the Word of God is the foundation of every authentic Christian life. Any fruitful spirituality has its roots in the reading, the study, and the meditation of the Bible. I perhaps seem to belabor an obvious point. However, I feel a strong fear when I notice that some religious groups substitute some devotions for the intelligent and demanding study of God's Word. This sort of study is at the same time full of nourishment. Here is Merton's testimony:

> Merely to set down some of the communicable meanings that can be found in a passage of Scripture is not to exhaust the true meaning or value of that passage. Every word that comes from the mouth of God is nourishment that feeds the soul with eternal life. *Non in solo pane vivit homo, sed in omni verbo quod procedit de ore Dei* [One does not live by bread alone, / but by every word that comes from the mouth of God]. Whether Scripture tells of David hiding from Saul in the mountains . . . or whether it tells about Jesus raising up the son of the widow of Naim . . . everywhere these are doors and windows opened into the same eternity and the most powerful communication of Scripture is the *insitum verbum*, the secret and inexpressible seed of contemplation planted in the depths of our soul and awakening it with an immediate and inexpressible contact with the Living Word, that we may adore him in Spirit and in Truth.[5]

★ ★ ★

5. Thomas Merton, *The Sign of Jonas* (New York: Harcourt, Brace and Company, 1953) 215.

Monastics do not make the vows of poverty and chastity as other religious do. It is not because these demands are foreign to them! But they are contained in a wider reality which is called *conversio* or *conversatio morum*, that is, conversion of one's manner of life, to which is added the vow of stability. Those who make their monastic profession tie themselves forever to a given community and commit themselves to a permanent conversion. This point is significant: the monastic profession concerns the entire life of monastics, so that they cannot reserve for themselves any exclusive domain. Even though the word monastic originally means solitary, today the etymology of the term (from the Greek *monos*, alone) is often explained by saying that monastics have brought singleness of purpose into their lives. Which is true.

"Repent and believe in the Good News," Jesus said. Monastics are those who, far from having reached perfection (Saint Benedict avoids this term), are constantly seeking conversion. Here again, is this not the program for any Christian life?

I believe that, in the last analysis, Christian life is conversion. Therefore, its only terminus is the shore of eternity.

By Way
of Conclusion

In the beginning of this work, I forbade myself to write a manual for the disciple's use. Readers must now understand better the reason for this decision of mine. A treatise on Christian life supposes a certain degree of exhaustiveness which I did not seek to attain. Thus, themes as essential as faith and hope have been hardly touched upon. The themes that have been treated have been approached from a certain angle, which I partially explained. As I said, I have been strongly influenced by a rather long stay at the Abbey of Tamié where I shared the life of the monks in its entirety. What I said about them in the preceding pages surely has not given any hint of any unwholesome "angelism." The men I met were thoroughly human, full of good qualities and defects; I have prayed and worked with them; on occasion I have had disagreements with them; and I do not doubt that sometimes I must have sorely tried their patience. In a word, we have tamed one another.

A short time before my departure from the monastery, I met a guest who had wandered into the enclosure and was asking me where the exit was. I answered humorously—a thing he probably was not in a mood to appreciate—that it was easier to enter a monastery than to get out of one. Which is the simple truth. If someone was to ask me what was the main benefit of my stay in a monastery, I would answer without any hesitation: learning to be a Christian. This could cause surprise. But it is true that life in community in the school of Saint Benedict "under a rule and an abbot" led me to perceive what a happy thing it is to be a Christian. It is this joy that I have wanted to share in these pages. They helped me to keep alive in me what the Ancients call the *memoria Dei* (the memory of God).

Often, one hears the question: "How can they stand it?" It is a good question, so good that monastics have the duty of asking it of themselves: *Friend, what have you come for?* (RB 60.3). And it is the answer that they voice which allows them not only to "stand it" but even to live "good days" (RB Prologue, 15). Monastics are God-seekers: "O God, you are my God, I seek you, / my soul thirsts for you" (Ps 63:1). There is no other answer, no other explanation, no other end to monastic life, which is a Christian life freed from every distraction, as I already have written.[1] The end they pursue and hope to reach is therefore also our own. Cassian describes it in the following terms:

> This will be the case when every love, every desire, every effort, every undertaking, every thought of ours, everything that we live, that we speak, that we breathe, will be God, and when that unity which the Father now has with the Son and which the Son has with the Father will be carried over into our understanding and our mind, so that, just as he loves us with a sincere and pure and indissoluble love, we too may be joined to him with a perpetual and inseparable love and so united with him that whatever we breathe, whatever we understand, whatever we speak, may be God. In him we shall attain, I say, to the end of which we spoke before, which the Lord longed to be fulfilled in us when he prayed: "That all may be one as we are one, I in them and you in me, that they themselves may also be made perfect in unity." And again: "Father, I wish that those whom you have given me may also be with me where I am."

---

1. See chapter 7, p. 34.

This then is the goal of the solitary, and this must be his whole intention—to deserve to possess the image of future blessedness in this body and as it were to begin to taste the pledge of that heavenly way of life and glory in this vessel."[2]

How can we reach this?

The last word of the Rule of Benedict enunciates a certainty: "You will arrive *(pervenies)*." On one condition formulated in the first word of the Rule: Listen carefully *(obsculta)*."

Listen carefully to the other, listen to the Word made flesh, listen to the Gospel. It is both quite simple and very complex. This is Christian life, provided one remembers that in the Benedictine as well as in the evangelical perspective, listening implies practice.

Listen carefully . . . and you will arrive.

Under God's protection (Deo protegente, pervenies).[3]

2. John Cassian, "Conference 10, On Prayer," in John Cassian, *The Conferences*, trans. Boniface Ramsey (New York: Paulist Press, 1997) 375–76.

3. *RB 1980: The Rule of St. Benedict*, ed. Timothy Fry (Collegeville, Minn.: Liturgical Press, 1981) 73.9.

Bibliography

Authors Cited

Aelred, of Rievaulx. *La vie de recluse [et] La prière pastorale.* Trans. Charles Dumont. Sources chrétiennes 76. Paris: Cerf, 1961.

Baud, Phillipe. *La ruche de Cîteaux: les plus belles pages des premiers Pères cisterciens.* Epiphanie: tradition monastique, Paris: Cerf, 1997.

Bernard, of Clairvaux. *Song of Songs.* 4 vols. Trans. Kilian Walsh and Irene Edmonds. Cistercian Fathers 4, 7, 31, 40. Kalamazoo, Mich.: Cistercian Publications, 1979–1983.

Cassian, John, *The Conferences.* Trans. Boniface Ramsey. New York: Paulist Press, 1997.

Christophe, moine de Tibhirine. *Le souffle du don: Journal de frère Christophe, moine de Tibhirine, 8 août 1993–19 mars 1996.* Paris: Bayard, 1999.

Guillerand, Augustin. *Voix cartusienne.* Saint-Maur: Parole et Silence, 2001.

Hémon, Philippe, Frère. "C'étaient mes frères, c'étaient des moines. . . ," in *Sept vies pour Dieu et l'Algérie.* Ed. Bruno Chenu. Paris: Bayard, 1996.

Huerre, Denis. *Letters to My Brothers and Sisters: Living by the Rule of St. Benedict.* Trans. Sylvester Houédard. Collegeville, Minn.: Liturgical Press, 1994.

Jérôme, Père. *L'art d'être disciple.* Paris: Le Serment, 1989.

Merton, Thomas. *La nuit privée d'étoiles.* Coll. Livre de Vie 2-3. Paris: Albin Michel, 1951.

——. *The Sign of Jonas.* New York: Harcourt, Brace and Company, 1953.

Michaux, Charles. *Traces de contemplation.* Signatures. Paris: Cerf, 1998.

Olivera, Bernardo. *How Far to Follow?: The Martyrs of Atlas.* Kalamazoo, Mich.: Cistercian Publications, 1997.

Quesnel, Michel. *L'éternité qui m'est offerte.* Paris: Desclée de Brouwer, 1998.

RB 1980: The Rule of St. Benedict. Ed. Timothy Fry and associate eds. Collegeville, Minn.: Liturgical Press, 1981.

William of Saint-Thierry. *Lettre aux frères du Mont-Dieu: lettre d'or.* Sources chrétiennes 223 Paris: Cerf, 1975.

——. *Le miroir de la foi.* Trans. Jean Déchanet. Sources chrétiennes 301. Paris: Cerf, 1982.

Suggested Reading

Benedictine Handbook, The. Collegeville, Minn.: Liturgical Press, 2003.

Derkse, Wil. *The Rule of Benedict for Beginners: Spirituality for Daily Life.* Trans. Martin Kessler. Collegeville, Minn.: Liturgical Press, 2003.

De Waal, Esther. *A Life-Giving Way: A Commentary on the Rule of St. Benedict.* Collegeville, Minn., Liturgical Press, 1995.

Kardong, Terrence. *Benedict's Rule: A Translation and Commentary.* Collegeville, Minn.: Liturgical Press, 1996.

Magrassi, Mariano. *Praying the Bible: An Introduction to* Lectio Divina. Trans. Edward Hagman. Collegeville, Minn.: Liturgical Press, 1998.

Romero, Mary Jane. *Seeking: A Paraphrase of the Rule of Saint Benedict with Commentary.* Collegeville, Minn.: Liturgical Press, 1972.

Rooney, Don. *Journeying with the Bible.* Collegeville, Minn.: Liturgical Press, 2005.

Skudlarek William, general ed. *The Continuing Quest for God: Monastic Spirituality in Tradition and Transition.* Collegeville, Minn.: Liturgical Press, 1982.

Tvedten, Benet. *A Share in the Kingdom: A Commentary on the Rule of St. Benedict for Oblates.* Collegeville, Minn.: Liturgical Press, 1989.